CAMPAIGN • 199

PHILIPPI 42 BC

The death of the Roman Republic

SI SHEPPARD

ILLUSTRATED BY STEVE NOON

Series editors Marcus Cowper and Nikolai Bogdanovic

First published in 2008 by Osprey Publishing
Midland House, West Way, Botley, Oxford OX2 0PH, UK
443 Park Avenue South, New York, NY 10016, USA
E-mail: info@ospreypublishing.com

ISBN 978 184603 265 3

Editorial: Ilios Publishing, Oxford, UK (www.iliospublishing.com)
Design: The Black Spot
Typeset in Sabon and Myriad Pro
Index by Alison Worthington
Originated by United Graphic Pte Ltd., Singapore
Cartography: The Map Studio
Bird's-eye view artworks: The Black Spot
Printed in China through Worldprint

08 09 10 11 12   10 9 8 7 6 5 4 3 2 1

A CIP catalogue record for this book is available from the British Library.

FOR A CATALOGUE OF ALL BOOKS PUBLISHED BY OSPREY MILITARY
AND AVIATION PLEASE CONTACT:

NORTH AMERICA
Osprey Direct, c/o Random House Distribution Center, 400 Hahn Road,
Westminster, MD 21157
E-mail: info@ospreydirect.com

ALL OTHER REGIONS
Osprey Direct UK, P.O. Box 140, Wellingborough, Northants, NN8 2FA, UK
E-mail: info@ospreydirect.co.uk

www.ospreypublishing.com

AUTHOR'S NOTE

Dedicated to Daniel Deudney: Mentor, Conlega, Amicus.

ARTIST'S NOTE

Readers may care to note that the original paintings from which the
colour plates in this book were prepared are available for private sale.
The Publishers retain all reproduction copyright whatsoever. All enquiries
should be addressed to:

Steve Noon,
50 Colchester Avenue,
Penylan,
Cardiff CF23 9BP,
UK

The Publishers regret that they can enter into no correspondence upon
this matter.

THE WOODLAND TRUST

Osprey Publishing are supporting the Woodland Trust, the UK's leading
woodland conservation charity, by funding the dedication of trees.

Key to military symbols

Army Group · Army · Corps · Division · Brigade · Regiment · Battalion · Company/Battery · Infantry · Artillery · Cavalry

Key to unit identification
Unit identifier · Parent unit · Commander · (+) with added elements · (−) less elements

CONTENTS

INTRODUCTION 5

CHRONOLOGY 13

OPPOSING COMMANDERS 16

OPPOSING ARMIES 20
Recruitment, organization and training . Combat . Politics

FROM MUTINA TO THE SECOND TRIUMVIRATE 28

THE ROAD TO PHILIPPI 38
Brutus's movements . Cassius's movements . The Republican consolidation of the east
Opposing plans

THE BATTLES OF PHILIPPI 50
The orders of battle . The opening moves . The First Battle of Philippi
The Second Battle of Philippi

AFTERMATH 79
The West: the Perusine War . The East: the Parthian Intervention

THE BATTLEFIELD TODAY 92

BIBLIOGRAPHY 93

INDEX 95

The Roman world on the ides of March, 44 BC

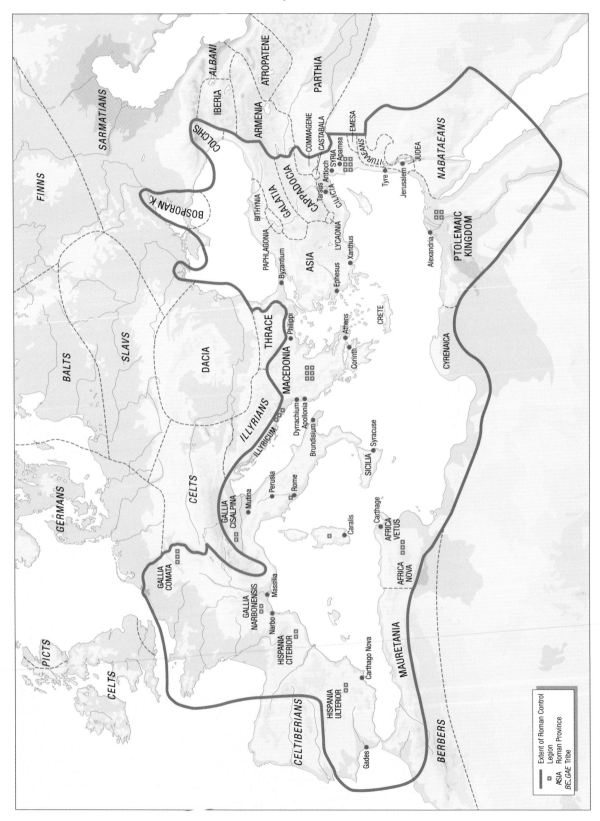

Extent of Roman Control
▫ Legion
ASIA Roman Province
BC. GAE Tribe

INTRODUCTION

This bust of Caesar artfully disguises the dictator's receding hairline. The sources relate that of all the decrees passed by a fawning and compliant Senate that most prized by Caesar was its granting him the right to wear the laurel wreath of a victorious general at his discretion. By 44 BC this had been superseded by a gold version. (Bildarchiv Preussischer Kulturbesitz/Art Resource, NY)

RIGHT
In defiance of the curse laid upon its ruins, one of Caesar's acts as dictator was to authorize the resettlement of Carthage, Rome's ancestral enemy, devastated at the conclusion of the Third Punic War a century earlier. From a 17th-century ceiling panel at Versailles. (Art Archive)

'Why, man, he doth bestride the narrow world like a Colossus.' With these words Shakespeare encapsulated the unprecedented authority of Julius Caesar at the end of the year 45 BC. He was the man who had accomplished the impossible; the man who had conquered Gaul, who had crossed the Channel and bridged the Rhine, who in the space of little more than four years of civil war had defeated Pompey the Great and every other opponent who dared challenge him in Italy, Spain, the Balkans, Asia Minor, Egypt and Africa. Now he was master of Rome and aspired to surpass Alexander's achievements in the east.

It was true that Caesar's writ did not hold sway throughout the entire Republic. Two men, at opposite ends of the Mediterranean, maintained the flickering flame of resistance. Caecilius Bassus, an adherent of Pompey who had fled to Tyre after Caesar's victory at Pharsalus, succeeded in inciting a revolt against the governor of Syria, Caesar's nephew Lucius, who was put to death by his own troops. Complementing the Roman legion he thus inherited by raising a vernacular legion, Bassus occupied the strongly fortified town of

This coin, in circulation on the ides of March, depicts Caesar in the vestments of the *pontifex maximus*, the high priest of Rome – hence the declaration in Ovid's *Fasti* that: 'all the daring criminals who in defiance of the gods, defiled the high priest's head, have fallen in merited death. Philippi is witness, and those whose scattered bones whiten its earth.' (Wayne Sayles)

Apamea, where he maintained himself for three years. He was first besieged by Antistius Vetus, who was forced to retire when Arabian and Parthian incursions came to the assistance of Bassus. Statius Murcus succeeded Vetus as governor with three legions, but he too was repulsed and was obliged to call on Marcius Crispus, the governor of Bithynia, who brought three more legions.

More seriously, in Spain Sextus Pompey, last heir to Pompey the Great, was still at large. A fugitive when Caesar left Spain, he had emerged as a guerilla leader with the surviving Pompeians, disaffected local peoples, and fugitive slaves flocking to his banner. The governor of Hispania Ulterior having failed to suppress this insurgency, Caesar replaced him in the spring of 44 BC with Asinius Pollio. The new governor was equally unsuccessful, being so badly worsted in one encounter he abandoned his *paludumentum*, the scarlet cloak of a general, to avoid being recognized as he fled. Sextus was hailed as *imperator* after this victory; with the force under his command having swollen to the equivalent of seven legions, he accepted the surrender of Carthago Nova.

These isolated redoubts were little more than irritants to the grand Caesarean project. Having mobilized 16 legions and 10,000 cavalry, the dictator would first strike against the Dacians on the far side of the Danube and then avenge the debacle at Carrhae in 53 BC by launching a full-scale invasion of Parthia.

Few authoritarian regimes have been as mild as that of Caesar, who sought reconciliation and consensus in the wake of the Civil War. Even his ostensible enemies had to admit to his generally benign nature. Nevertheless, the institutions of the Republic were becoming hollow, maintaining the illusion of the traditional checks and balances of the constitution but in fact responding entirely to the will of Caesar. The latter held the title of *pontifex maximus*, the chief religious magistrate of Rome, and, having already assumed the office of dictator for ten years, was named *dictator perpetuo* and *parens patriae*, father of the state, early in 44 BC.

His birthday became a public holiday, and the month Quintilis was renamed July in his honour. A Julian college of priests was created and a temple dedicated to his clemency. His cult was to be the charge of a new order of priest; his chief lieutenant Mark Antony was named as the first of these.

Senators in ceremonial regalia. Caesar appointed many of his supporters to this body, swelling its size while marginalizing its oversight of his administration. (Alinari, Art Resource, NY)

For over a century Romans had enjoyed being labelled gods by the peoples they subjugated in the east, but this was introducing divine authority into Rome itself.

Caesar took to wearing the purple tunic and toga of a triumphant general to festivals and meetings of state. By 44 BC he was appearing in public crowned with the laurel wreath of victory fashioned in gold.

Every king needs a queen, and in late 46 BC Caesar's erstwhile mistress, Queen Cleopatra VII of Egypt, and his bastard son by her, Caesarion, had taken up residence in one of the dictator's estates on the far bank of the Tiber. Caesar had a gold statue of her erected in the Temple of Venus Genetrix, the centrepiece of his new forum.

On 15 February 44 BC Rome celebrated the festival of the Lupercal. At this moment Antony, now consul, presented Caesar with a royal diadem, urging him to take it and declare himself king. When Caesar refused, the crowd cheered; the roars of acclamation grew louder when Caesar refused a second offer and ordered the diadem to be placed in the Temple of Jupiter, because here was Rome's only king. The spectacle was obviously staged to publicly demonstrate Caesar's lack of interest in royal titles, but its only effect was to further energize rumour and speculation about his ultimate ambition being the restoration of the monarchy.

A conspiracy against Caesar emerged that ultimately incorporated dozens of senators with a broad spectrum of motivations, from genuine loyalty to the Republic to personal jealousy. Most, like Marcus Brutus and his brother-in-law Gaius Cassius, were conservative members of the *optimates* faction who had aligned with Pompey and owed their titles, and indeed their lives, to Caesar's *clementia* after his defeat; but some, such as Decimus Brutus and Caius Trebonius, had been given their military commands by Caesar and had proved loyal subordinates during his Gallic and Civil wars.

Caesar planned to leave Rome to take command in the field on 18 March and had made preparations for a long absence, the public offices and magistracies having been allocated for the next three years. If the conspirators were going to strike they had to do so before Caesar left the city. The most favourable opportunity would arise on the ides of March – the 15th of the month – when the Senate would meet in the curia of Pompey's Theatre and Caesar would be isolated, having dismissed his bodyguard after the Senate swore an oath of loyalty to him.

In the event, bad omens nearly kept Caesar at home on the ides, but he was eventually cajoled into attending. After Trebonius lured away Antony the other conspirators unsheathed their daggers and hacked Caesar to death.

The conspirators had thought to receive the *laudes* of the Senate, but the only response of the conscript fathers was panicked flight. Confronted by the empty seats of their colleagues the conspirators walked to the Capitol, carrying on a pole the cap granted to a freed slave; thus they symbolized the freedom they had restored to Rome. Caesar's body was left where it had fallen; later, three of his slaves collected it and bore it to his house in a litter.

Some opportunists jumped on board the conspirators' bandwagon, most notably Cicero's son-in-law Publius Dolabella, who peremptorily seized the fasces and the insignia of the consulship Caesar had promised him. In general, however, the public reaction was one of stunned dismay. The conspirators squandered whatever political and moral capital their act had endowed them with.

The initiative swung to Antony, who, after spending the night in hiding, on the 16th secured from Caesar's wife Calpurnia the dictator's papers. After

TOP
The rhythm of life in Rome had been marked since the foundation of the Republic by the participation of the citizens in the political process, celebrated in this coin depicting the simple act of casting a ballot. (American Numismatic Society)

BOTTOM
Marcus Brutus served as a moneyer in 54 BC; this coin commemorates his ancestor, the L. Junius Brutus who established the Republic in 509 BC, showing him walking in procession, led by an *accensus* and flanked by lictors. (American Numismatic Society)

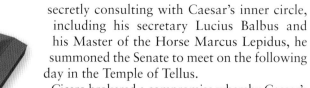

secretly consulting with Caesar's inner circle, including his secretary Lucius Balbus and his Master of the Horse Marcus Lepidus, he summoned the Senate to meet on the following day in the Temple of Tellus.

Cicero brokered a compromise whereby Caesar's acts and appointments would remain in effect but his assassins would receive amnesty. Even so, the latter would not descend from the Capitol until Antony and Lepidus had offered their sons as hostages. That night Brutus dined with Lepidus and Cassius with Antony.

In a further manifestation of the spirit of reconciliation the Senate voted a public funeral for Caesar, which was held on the 18th. This was the occasion Antony seized to mobilize the urban population. He had the honours voted to Caesar by the Senate enumerated, along with the oath taken by every senator to preserve his life; he listed the contents of Caesar's will, including the gift of public gardens and a donative of 75 denarii to every citizen; and finally he displayed Caesar's purple cloak, now rent by the daggers of the conspirators and disfigured with his blood. This sparked the emotional catharsis that had been numbed for the past three days. In a frenzy of grief the people tore apart the forum and cremated their Ceasar on a makeshift pyre.

Antony used the momentum generated by this spontaneous outpouring of loyalty to Caesar's memory to solidify his control over Rome. One by one the conspirators abandoned the city, starting with Brutus and Cassius on 13 April. Others departed to take up their provincial commands – Decimus to Gallia Cisalpina, Trebonius to Asia, Tillius Cimber to Bithynia. In addition, after being elected to succeed Caesar as *pontifex maximus* Lepidus, who had been charged with negotiations aimed at the reconciliation of Sextus, left for Spain.

Antony was careful not to disturb the delicate political consensus. As a gesture of good faith to the conservatives he even abolished the office of dictator. However, power rested not with the Senate but with the legions, and Antony had to attend to their needs first. He was absent from Rome for a month in the provinces administering the allotment of lands and the founding of military colonies. When he returned he found a new challenge had emerged from an unexpected quarter.

Gaius Octavian was born on 23 September 63 BC, the grandson of Caesar's sister Julia. Coming of age during the Civil War he yearned to serve with his illustrious great-uncle, but his youth and frail health (a perennial liability throughout his career) prevented him from playing any part other than arriving in Spain after Caesar's final victory there. The dictator sensed enough in the young man to adopt him and name him his chief heir in the will he deposited with the Vestal Virgins upon his return to Rome on 13 September 45 BC.

Octavian was studying at Apollonia when his mother Atia notified him of Caesar's demise and urged him to join her in Rome: 'you must now play the man,' she added; 'consider what ought to be done, and act.' Octavian sailed to Brundisium (Brindisi) and then journeyed to Rome, arriving in early May. He quickly set about reconstituting Caesar's network of military and political patronage.

Shortly after Antony returned to the city on 18 May he granted an audience to Octavian, who demanded his inheritance from Caesar. The

Pompey's Theatre. The Curia Pompeia at the far end of the peristyle colonnade, where the Senate met on the ides of March, is not depicted in this reconstruction. The conspirators had infiltrated gladiators into the games scheduled for that day as a contingency against the attempt on Caesar's life going awry. (King's Visualization Lab)

consul curtly dismissed him. Who was this boy who presumed to claim the mantle of Caesar when Antony had served for more than 10 years at the side of the dictator in both Gallic and Civil Wars? Antony no doubt reminded him that during their journey back from Spain in 45 BC it was he who had shared the lead carriage with Caesar while Octavian had travelled in a second coach with Decimus.

Nevertheless, Octavian's presence upset Antony's delicate political tightrope act because Caesar's adopted son represented an alternative focus for the smouldering rage of the veterans who were dismayed Antony had done nothing to avenge Caesar's murder. Antony began to act in a more overtly authoritarian manner. On 1 June he obtained a plebiscite from the assembly that gave him, in lieu of the Macedonian province previously assigned to him, Gallia Cisalpina and Gallia Comata for a five-year term.

TOP LEFT
Nothing remains above ground of Pompey's Theatre. The surviving subterranean structures offer an interesting ambience for the ristorante *Da Pancrazio*. (Courtesy Linda and Steve Brudz)

TOP RIGHT
The dagger (*pugio*) each conspirator smuggled into Pompey's Theatre, concealed in the carry-case for their writing stylus, must have been of a similar type to this example recovered from the ruins of Pompeii. (AAA Collection)

LEFT
While disappearing beneath a swarm of thrusting and slashing blades, Caesar is unlikely to have struck the dramatic pose depicted in *The Death of Julius Caesar* by Vincenzo Camuccini. Several senators, including Brutus, were wounded in the frenzied mêlée; according to the historian Nicolaus, 'It looked as if they were fighting over Caesar.' (Scala, Art Resource, NY)

The conspirators left Caesar with 23 wounds in his body lying at the feet of a statue of his rival Pompey. *The Death of Caesar*, by Jean Leon Gerome. (Bridgeman)

This measure not only defied the convention that it was the Senate that decided provincial appointments, it almost certainly meant civil war, since Decimus was unlikely to surrender his legions without a fight. Antony's consular colleague Dolabella, who had turned his coat again, received a five-year command in Syria. Of the six legions in Macedonia, Dolabella was to receive one, Antony the other five.

Antony was concerned about Brutus and Cassius. If they remained in Italy they might serve as the focus for opposition to his regime; conversely, they could not be allowed to obtain power through a prestigious appointment in the provinces. On 5 June Antony directed the Senate to assign Brutus and Cassius the demeaning task of supervising the grain export to Rome from Asia and Sicily respectively. Three days later the Republicans – Cicero, Cassius, Brutus with his wife Porcia and mother Servilia – convened at Antium (Anzio). Cassius stated bluntly: 'To Sicily I will not go. Am I to accept an insult as a favour?' Servilia, who had been Caesar's mistress, promised to intervene, and on 1 August the Senate assigned the provinces of Crete to Brutus and Cyrene to Cassius.

These token appointments only further inflamed the pride of the leading conspirators. They wrote to Antony on 4 August advising him 'our freedom means more to us than your friendship' and warning him to 'bear in mind, not only the length of Caesar's life, but the brevity of his reign.' Both men subsequently departed Italy to seek their own fortunes in the east.

Meanwhile, Antony's relations with Octavian continued to deteriorate. Octavian had strengthened his position at the end of July when he won over a major section of the populace by sponsoring games, the *Ludi Victoriae Caesaris*, ostensibly honouring Venus but in reality glorifying Caesar. The appearance of a comet at the height of the festival convinced many of Caesar's divinity and by extension that fortune smiled on his adopted son. When one of the tribunes died, Octavian hoped to be elected in his place. Antony opposed the measure on the grounds Octavian was disqualified by being both too young to be eligible and a patrician. Shortly afterwards he arrested a number of the veterans comprising his bodyguard on the grounds they had been suborned – by Octavian he hinted – to assassinate him.

Sensing the possibility of restoring the independence of the Senate by pitting the two rivals for Caesar's estate against each other, Cicero, who had abandoned Rome in despair and had taken ship for Athens, returned to the city. He undertook to play the role of mentor to Octavian while isolating Antony with a series of ferocious addresses, the *Philippics*.

Power, however, rested in the sword not in speeches. Whoever controlled the armies controlled the Republic, a fact made manifest when four of the Macedonian legions – the II, IV, Martian and XXXV – were shipped across the Adriatic to Italy. On 9 October Antony set out for to Brundisium to greet them and to arrange the details for their northwards march. He received an unexpectedly hostile reception from the legions, which, having been suborned by agents of Octavian, upbraided him for continuing to indulge Caesar's murderers. Antony offered to buy their loyalty, but Octavian had already made the higher bid. When the legionaries began to disperse, Antony forced them back into line by having the ringleaders arrested and summarily executed. He then ordered them to march to Arminium (Rimini) while he returned to Rome.

Octavian meanwhile proceeded to the colonies of Calatia and Casilinum in Campania and persuaded upwards of 3,000 of the veterans of Caesar's legions VII and VIII to march with him on Rome, distributing a 500 denarii reward among the soldiers, with a promise of 5,000 more if they were victorious. Octavian occupied the forum on 10 November, but the coup failed and his support evaporated. He withdrew northwards into Etruria and established a base at Arretium (Arezzo). Antony summoned a meeting of the Senate for 24 November with the intent of having Octavian branded as an enemy of the state.

Just as it seemed Octavian's premature tilt at power would result in his destruction, the wheel of fortune again turned in his favour. While marching north along the Adriatic seaboard the Martian legion declared for Caesar's heir, turned westward along the Via Valeria, and took up station in the fortress colony of Alba Fucens near modern Avezzano, overlooking the Fucine Lake in central Italy. The Martians were soon joined by the IV Legion. Antony hurriedly confronted them, but they ignored his entreaties and spurned his miserly bribes.

Antony responded by further raising the stakes. On the evening of 28 November, when the Senate could not legally meet, 13 provinces were assigned by lot – the lots being manipulated, as Cicero hinted, so that the key assignments were secured by those loyal to Antony, including his brother Gaius, who obtained Macedonia. Trebonius was stripped of Asia, his entitlement under the acts of Caesar notwithstanding; thus the amnesty which had maintained the fragile peace since the ides of March was broken. Antony promptly marched for Gallia Cisalpina with the remaining Macedonian legions, the II and XXXV, as well as the newly reconstituted V legion and whatever veterans and recruits he had succeeded in enlisting. He sent his legate, Publius Ventidius, into Campania and Lucania to recruit additional troops from the Caesarean veterans of legions VII, VIII and IX colonized there.

Decimus, who had raised two new legions, doubling the total under his command, and blooded them in a series of campaigns against the Alpine tribes, refused to hand over the province. This was illegal, but his action was

The rostrum in the Forum of Rome. From this platform the rival cases, pro and anti-Caesar, were presented to the citizens. (Felix Just, S.J.)

justified by Cicero, who advised him that 'in safeguarding the liberty and welfare of the Roman people you must not wait to be authorized by a Senate which is not yet free.' Decimus decided against confrontation. In order to leave the choice of initiating the first act of violence to Antony he fortified Mutina (Modena), provisioning the city by slaughtering and smoking his transport cattle. After occupying Bononia (Bologna) Antony commenced laying siege to Mutina.

Octavian shadowed Antony with the Martian, IV, VII, and VIII legions. At the start of the new year, emboldened by Cicero's fifth *Philippic*, the Senate voted to grant Octavian joint command with the two incoming consuls, Aulus Hirtius and Gaius Pansa, against Antony. The Senate also committed itself to pay the donative Octavian had promised the IV and Martian legions, discharge all the troops Octavian had raised at the end of the campaign, exempt their sons from military service, and grant land to the soldiers upon demobilization.

Senatorial moderates still insisted on arriving at a compromise and succeeded in appointing an embassy to confer with Antony and seek the terms under which he would be prepared to scale down the crisis. Antony declared he was willing to surrender Gallia Cisalpina, but wished to retain Gallia Comata for five years with the three legions under his command and the three Ventidius was recruiting.

When the embassy returned at the beginning of February with this proposal the senatorial moderates were able to water down the declaration of war against Antony to a declaration of *tumultus*, or civil disorder. However, events were quickly spiralling out of the Senate's control.

While Pansa was tasked with conscripting troops and collecting newly levied taxes in Italy, Hirtius had immediately marched north to link up with Octavian, who was camped at Forum Cornelium, 53km south-east of Bononia on the Aemilian Way. Hirtius advanced a further 21km to Claterna (Quaderna), from which he evicted Antony's garrison. After taking possession of the city Hirtius then had to defend it against a counterattack. 'A battle was fought,' he wrote to his colleague Pansa, 'The cavalry were routed… A good many men were slain.' They were the first deaths of the second civil war.

CHRONOLOGY

44 BC

March 15   Caesar assassinated.

March 17   The Senate extends amnesty to the assassins.

March 18   Antony's funeral oration.

Late March   Octavian leaves Apollonia for Italy; Lepidus leaves Rome for his provinces.

Early April   Passage of the *lex Antonia de dictatura in perpetuum tollenda*; the assassins leave Rome for Campania.

Mid-April   Dolabella and Antony assigned Syria and Macedonia respectively for the following year.

Late April   Antony leaves for Campania.

Early May   Octavian arrives in Rome and claims his inheritance.

May 18   Antony returns to Rome; he meets with Octavian shortly thereafter.

June 1   Antony secures by plebiscite the exchange of Macedonia for Cisalpine Gaul while retaining command of the Macedonian legions.

June 5   Brutus and Cassius granted charge of the grain supply.

Mid-June   Cicero leaves for Athens.

July 6–13   *Ludi Apollinares.*

July 20–30   *Ludi Victoriae Caesaris.*

August 1   Brutus and Cassius assigned Crete and Cyrene.

August 31   Cicero returns to Rome.

Late August   Brutus leaves for Athens.

September 2   Cicero delivers the first *Phillipic* and leaves Rome shortly thereafter.

Early September   Cassius leaves for Syria.

October 5/6   Alleged attempt by Octavian to assassinate Antony.

October 9   Antony leaves for Brundisium to meet the troops arriving from Macedonia; Octavian leaves for Campania.

November 10   Octavian enters Rome; he departs for Etruria shortly thereafter.

November 24   Antony, shortly after arriving in Rome, fails to appear at a Senate meeting he had convened.

November 28   The Senate reassigns the provinces in Antony's favour.

Late November   Antony departs for Cisalpine Gaul.

December 9   Cicero returns to Rome.

December 20	Cicero delivers the third *Phillipic*, convincing the Senate to revoke Antony's distribution of the provinces.	**April 27**	The Senate declares Antony a *hostis*; appoints Sextus Pompey naval command; confirms Cassius as proconsul of Syria.
Late December	Decimus, refusing to yield Cisalpine Gaul to Antony, is besieged at Mutina.	**May 29**	Lepidus joins with Antony.
43 BC		**June 30**	The Senate unanimously declares Lepidus a *hostis*.
January 1–4	Hirtius and Pansa take office as consuls; the Senate confirms Octavian as propraetor with joint responsibility for the campaign against Antony; Hirtius and Octavian mobilize troops for the march to Mutina while Pansa continues the levy; embassy dispatched to treat with Antony.	**Early July**	Octavian sends an embassy of soldiers to the Senate to demand a consulship; he is rebuffed.
		Mid-August	Octavian marches on Rome.
		September 22	Octavian takes office as consul.
Early 43 BC	Gaius Antonius is defeated by Brutus at Dyrrachium; Brutus proceeds to secure his position in Thrace and Macedonia during spring and summer. Cassius inherits the legions of Murcus, Crispus and Bassus at Apamea; over the course of spring and summer he campaigns in Syria and defeats Dolabella at Laodicea.	**Late September**	Having provided for Caesar's murderers to be outlawed under the *lex Pedia* Octavian, charged with the campaign against Lepidus and Antony, marches for Gaul; Sextus Pompey, falsely condemned under the *lex Pedia*, leaves Massilia.
February 1–3	The Senate's embassy returns with Antony's demands; *tumultus* declared; after news of Gaius Antonius' defeat reaches Rome Cicero successfully moves that Brutus be confirmed as proconsul of Macedonia, Illyria and Greece.	**Mid-November**	Formation of the Triumvirate outside Bononia; the Triumvirs march on Rome.
		November 27	The Triumvirate is ratified in Rome by the *lex Titia*; proscriptions declared.
		December 7	Cicero murdered.
March 19	Pansa marches to join Hirtius and Octavian.	**Late 43 BC**	Brutus and Cassius meet at Smyrna to coordinate their strategy for the upcoming campaign season; Sextus Pompey arrives in Sicily.
March 20	Dispatches from Lepidus and Plancus urging peace with Antony are read to the Senate; Cicero delivers his thirteenth *Philippic* in response.	**42 BC**	
		January 1	Lepidus and Plancus take office as consuls.
April 14	The battle at Forum Gallorum.	**Early 42 bc**	Brutus campaigns successfully in Lycia; Cassius occupies Rhodes.
April 21	The battle at Mutina.		
April 22	Antony raises the siege of Mutina and marches north for the Alps.	**Mid-July**	Brutus and Cassius meet at Sardis in preparation for the march to Philippi.
April 23	Octavian snubs Decimus.		

August	Saxa and Norbanus dispatched to Thrace in advance of Antony and Octavian.	**40** BC	
		January 1	Calvinus and Pollio take office as consuls.
Early September	Brutus and Cassius arrive at the Hellespont; defeat of Salvidienus by Sextus Pompey.	January	Siege of Perusia.
		February	Surrender of Lucius Antonius.
Mid-September	Brutus and Cassius drive Saxa and Norbanus back into Macedonia and occupy Philippi; Antony and Octavian cross the Adriatic and advance to Philippi.	Spring	Antony leaves Alexandria; after receiving news of the outcome at Perusia while en route to Phoenicia he sets sail for Italy meeting envoys of Sextus Pompey in Athens; Octavian marches to Transalpine Gaul to take command of the legions there after the death of Calenus; he marries Scribonia, mother-in-law of Sextus Pompey.
October 3	First battle of Philippi; defeat of Octavian by Brutus; defeat of Cassius by Antony; suicide of Cassius; annihilation of Triumvirs' reinforcements under Calvinus while crossing the Adriatic by Republican fleet under Murcus and Ahenobarbus.		
		Summer	Antony besieges Brundisium; death of Fulvia; capture of Sardinia by Menas; mediation of Cocceius between Antony and Octavian.
October 23	Second battle of Philippi; defeat of Brutus by Antony and Octavian; suicide of Brutus.	October	Antony and Octavian come to an agreement at Brundisium and return to Rome to settle the situation there; Sextus Pompey renews his depredations.
Late October	Redistribution of the provinces by Antony and Octavian.		
41 BC		November	Antony marries Octavia.
		39 BC	
January 1	Lucius Antonius and Servilius take office as consuls.	January 1	Censorinus and Calvisius take office as consuls.
Early 41 BC	Antony winters in Athens; Octavian returns to Rome to oversee land allotments to the veterans and suppress Sextus Pompey.	Summer	Antony, Octavian and Sextus Pompey reach a settlement at Misenum.
Mid–late 41 BC	Antony travels to Ephesus in the spring; he meets Cleopatra in Cilicia; campaigns in Asia Minor, Syria and Palestine; winters in Alexandria with Cleopatra.		
December	The escalating conflict pitting Octavian against Lucius Antonius and Fulvia over land allotments to the veterans erupts into armed confrontation.		

OPPOSING COMMANDERS

Mark Antony was at the peak of his powers during the Philippi campaign. He was never more dangerous than during a crisis; on the battlefield he was a determined and resourceful adversary. Conversely, he was at his most vulnerable when burdened with the torpor of administration; he never mastered the arts of bureaucratic infighting and political intrigue. (Alinari/Art Resource, NY)

Marcus Junius Brutus, who was in his 37th year at Philippi, is habitually depicted as embodying the moral centre of the Republican cause. As such he is often portrayed as an almost other-worldly character, one divorced from the harsh realities of both politics and military command; typically, Plutarch relates that 'Brutus did not so much rely upon his forces, as upon his own virtue,' and for this reason, he 'was esteemed by the people, beloved by his friends, admired by the best men, and hated not by his enemies themselves. For he was a man of a singularly gentle nature.'

To a degree, these accounts overstate the case. It is true that upon his arrival in Athens Brutus relied upon the power of his moral authority to raise an army, but once enough volunteers had gathered under his banner he exhibited decisive initiative and skill while sweeping the Balkans clear of Antony's legates and in pacifying Thrace. Campaigning in Lycia he displayed a harder edge, ruthlessly subduing the region. Upon investing Xanthus, Brutus divided his army into day and night watches, 'hurrying and cheering them on as if for prizes,' according to Dio, who adds he 'spared neither zeal nor labour' during the course of the siege, which culminated in the effective liquidation of the population.

However, although Brutus was consistently successful in small to medium-scale theatre engagements he was a failure when circumstances left him in sole command of a major operation. To the last, there is no questioning his personal courage; at the second battle of Philippi, Dio says that he 'all the while performed all that was possible for an expert general and valiant soldier' to achieve victory. But in the final analysis the defining trait of his leadership was his ultimate failure to impose his authority over the men under his command.

His army pre-empted his order to advance and spontaneously charged during the first battle; the combined Republican force under his command forced him into the second battle against his better judgement. Appian sources the disaffection of the Republican army, forced to abide by his Fabian strategy after the first battle, to his inability to command the respect of his men:

> Brutus himself was the cause of these murmurs, being of a gentle and kindly disposition toward all – not like Cassius, who had been austere and imperious in every way, for which reason the army obeyed his orders promptly, not interfering with his authority, and not criticising them when they had learned them. But in the case of Brutus they expected nothing else than to share the command with him on account of his mildness of temper.

This aspect of Brutus's character, which went so far towards cementing his reputation as 'the noblest Roman of them all,' was a fatal flaw in a general.

It was the curious destiny of **Gaius Cassius Longinus** to prove a vigorous and resourceful commander in a succession of losing causes. He enters history as a quaestor on the staff of Crassus during the ill-fated invasion of Parthia; his well-informed tactical advice being consistently ignored, the Roman force was annihilated at Carrhae in 53 BC. Cassius rallied the survivors and for the next two years governed the province of Syria as proquaestor, repelling repeated Parthian incursions. In the final encounter he marshalled only his cavalry, having posted infantry in hiding on rough ground in the rear. When his cavalry fell back he drew the Parthians into the ambush prepared for them and slaughtered them, including their commander, Osaces.

Cassius sided with the *optimates* upon the outbreak of the Civil War. Commanding a naval squadron for Pompey he wiped out more than half of Caesar's fleet. A leading figure in the conspiracy against Caesar, his experience and reputation subsequently helped consolidate the entire east for the Republican cause.

The name of Cassius has been inseparably paired with that of Brutus for more than 2,000 years, and historians have tended to exaggerate their dominant character traits in order to explain their motivations and ultimate fates. Cassius typically is portrayed as the warrior to contrast against Brutus as the statesman. According to Paterculus, for example, 'Cassius was as much the better general as Brutus was the better man. Of the two, one would rather have Brutus as a friend, but would stand more in fear of Cassius as an enemy. The one had more vigour, the other more virtue. As it was better for the state to have Caesar rather than Antony as emperor, so, had Brutus and Cassius been the conquerors, it would have been better for it to be ruled by Brutus rather than by Cassius.'

The judgement of Plutarch that Cassius 'desired to command rather by fear than love' perhaps encapsulates the difference between his style and that of Brutus. Cassius was successful in instilling discipline among the men under

Gaius Cassius represents the archetypal warrior-politician of the Roman Republic, alternating military service in foreign and domestic wars with provincial and urban office. He has traditionally been depicted as the cynical foil to the romantic Brutus, but although undeniably ruthless he never ceased to believe that 'In war the greatest hope lies in the justice of one's cause.' (Courtesy Montreal Museum of Fine Art)

his command, for example after the fall of Rhodes, when he threatened with death any of his legionaries who resorted to violence or plunder, while Brutus never fully imposed his authority over the men who rallied to his banner. This dichotomy is hinted at in a vignette of Frontinus, who relates that on one occasion when the Republican armies were marching through Macedonia it was Brutus who arrived first at a stream but the troops of Cassius were the first in constructing a bridge and in effecting a passage.

A dissolute youth who fled to Greece to escape his creditors, while studying in Athens, **Marcus Antonius** (Mark Antony) was summoned by Aulus Gabinius, proconsul of Syria, to take part in the campaigns against Aristobulus in Judea, and in support of Ptolemy XII in Egypt. In 54 BC he joined Caesar's staff in Gaul and later served his interests in Rome in the offices of quaestor, augur, and finally tribune of the plebs. When Caesar seized Rome he appointed Antony Master of the Horse, effectively his right-hand man. Antony ran Pompey's naval blockade to bring reinforcements to Caesar in the Balkans and commanded the dictator's left wing at Pharsalus.

Antony was consistently at his best in a crisis, but whenever he was entrusted with executive office the outcome was always disastrous. Rome spiralled into chaos when Caesar left it in Antony's hands, but the two were later reconciled and Caesar chose Antony as his colleague for the consulship in 44 BC. It was in this role that Antony outmanoeuvred the conspirators after the ides, only to drive Octavian into the arms of the Senate and find himself a year after delivering Caesar's funeral oration declared an enemy of the state and on the run in the wake of his defeat at Mutina. 'But it was his character in calamities to be better than at any other time,' Plutarch writes 'Antony, in misfortune, was most nearly a virtuous man.' With no funds, no supplies, no allies, and reduced to giving his soldiers bark to use as shields, he rallied the men who followed him into exile, 'drinking foul water and feeding on wild fruits and roots,' according to Plutarch, who adds that in their passage over the Alps they 'lived upon creatures that no one before had ever been willing to touch.'

Having won over the legions of Gaul and Spain, Antony proved willing to compromise with his rival Octavian in order to concentrate on the common enemy. Although ostensibly sharing a joint command, he emerged from the Philippi campaign with tremendously enhanced prestige; it was his tactical initiatives that provoked both the first battle, in which his success stood as a vivid contrast to the utter failure of Octavian, and the second battle, where as Plutarch relates, 'Antony was in everything, and attacked everywhere,' eliminating the Republican threat once and for all.

Typically however, once this crisis had passed Antony's attention shifted to the pleasures of the flesh rather than affairs of state; while the East was being overrun by the Parthians and the West erupted in renewed war, Antony drifted between them, only intervening at the 11th hour and settling for another compromise with Octavian that left the Roman world more evenly divided between them than ever.

Antony was a soldier's soldier, but his ultimate station was as a loyal subordinate to a dominant personality, a character trait Cleopatra would take full advantage of.

On the first day of the New Year in 42 BC the Senate enrolled Caesar in the pantheon of Rome; his adopted son and designated heir could now style himself *divi filius*, the son of a god. In reality, **Gaius Julius Caesar Octavianus** was of a respectable but undistinguished family of the equestrian order (his father had been governor of Macedonia) and had inherited none of his illustrious grand-uncle's military genius. Still a teenager on the ides of March he had no experience either of battle or of commanding men.

Although the historians of the imperial era may have exaggerated Octavian's direct contribution to the downfall of the Republic, he does appear to have, within his limitations, attempted to play the part of the warlord demanded of him. According to Suetonius, during the battle of Mutina 'all agree that he played the part not only of a leader, but of a soldier as well, and that, in the thick of the fight, when the eagle-bearer of his legion was sorely wounded, he shouldered the eagle and carried it for some time.'

Recurring bouts of debilitating illness undermined Octavian's attempts to impose his authority during the campaign against the Republicans. It was only by a supreme effort of will that he was able to take command of his legions at Philippi at all, being described as so ill he could barely stand while wearing armour. Not that his presence counted for much; his camp was sacked in the first battle and he only survived by seeking shelter in the neighbouring swamp. His role in the second battle was a subordinate one; Plutarch states bluntly that Octavian 'did nothing worth relating, and all the success and victory were Antony's.'

Antony's star was in such ascendance in the wake of Philippi that Octavian could not induce the veteran troops under his command to take the field against him and had to watch, impotent, as the siege of Brundisium dragged on. Yet somehow Octavian was able to negotiate both the snake pit of Roman politics and the travails of civil war and emerge on equal terms with Antony. His intelligence, ambition, and, above all, the name Caesar had bequeathed him, all contributed to his unlikely perseverance. Perhaps his key asset was his ability to delegate tasks that were beyond his capacity to qualified subordinates, such as Marcus Agrippa. In the long term it was this ability to engender and reciprocate loyalty that would enable his ultimate triumph.

The overriding priority for Sextus Pompey during the terminal Republican period was recognition of his patrimony. This coin emphasizes his desire to establish his legitimacy by featuring portraits of his father, Pompey the Great, and his brother, Gnaeus, both hounded to their deaths by Caesar. (American Numismatic Society)

OPPOSING ARMIES

RECRUITMENT, ORGANIZATION AND TRAINING

Forming the core of both armies at Philippi were the legions that by the terminal Republic period had achieved a standardized template honed by centuries of imperial expansion. Each legionary was armed with sword (*gladius*), spear/javelin (*pilum*) and dagger (*pugio*) and protected by shield (*scutum*), helmet, and mail armour.

Standardized training, no less than standardized weapons, was the key to forging the fighting quality of the Roman military machine. Combat exercise centred on a shadow duel with a post set in the ground at man height. Recruits would be handed round bucklers woven with willows, twice as heavy as the shields used in the field, and wooden swords double the weight of the *gladius*. They would work out with these dummy weapons at the post both morning and afternoon. The recruit would be expected to alternate targeting the head, flanks, and thighs of his simulated opponent.

In particular, recruits were taught not to cut but to thrust with their swords. This was for two reasons. First, a stroke with the edges seldom kills, as the

The corporate structure of the Roman army was largely formalized by the terminal Republic period with units now institutionalized as opposed to being raised on an ad-hoc basis. This inscription identifies the IX cohort of legio X Fretensis, literally 'of the sea strait', a cognomen it won in 36 BC at the Battle of Naulochus, which took place near the Straits of Messina, the *Fretum Siculum*. (Author's collection)

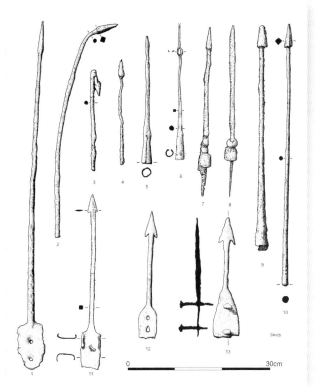

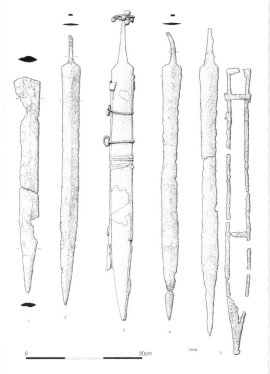

vital parts of the body are defended both by the bones and armour, while a stab wound is generally fatal. Second, a slashing motion exposes the right arm and side, while a thrust can be delivered from under cover of a shield, 'and the adversary receives the point before he sees the sword', Vegetius counsels.

Long after basic training concluded, drill would remain an endemic feature of a legionary's life in the service, its intensity stopping just short of actual combat in the veteran units. Appian notes that during the course of their exercises at Alba Fucens the IV and Martian legions formed up opposite each other 'and unsparingly did everything one does in a real battle except kill.'

Next to weapons drill the most important aspect of recruit training was basic instruction in the construction and maintenance of the camp. Vegetius asserts there could be 'no part of discipline so necessary and useful' as this skill. The capacity to quickly and efficiently construct a fortified camp, laid out in a grid pattern according to a standardized template, in hostile terrain was one of the distinguishing hallmarks of Roman warfare and vital to her expansion at ever greater distances from her Italian heartland.

Livy described the camp as 'the soldier's second homeland [*patria altera*] – its rampart serves as his city walls, and his tent is the soldier's hearth and home [*domus ac penates*].' The environment in which they operated while on campaign defined unit cohesion at the most essential level for the legionaries. Their commanders might refer to them as *commilito*, 'fellow soldier', but they called each other *contubernales*, 'tent-mates'. The ramparts they erected, surrounded by ditch (*fossa*), dyke (*agger*) and palisade (*vallum*), did not accord shelter merely to the combat troops, however; a large number of slaves, *calones*, were attached to a legion, many men having at least one personal slave attendant, and the presence of camp followers, *lixae*, was

TOP LEFT
The *pila* was the primary missile weapon of the legionary but could be kept in hand for use under certain scenarios, for example to repulse a cavalry charge. (Courtesy M.C. Bishop)

TOP RIGHT
Centuries of field testing refined the Roman sword, the *gladius*, into a straight and double-edged cut-and-thrust weapon approximately 60cm long with a V-shaped tip. (Courtesy M.C. Bishop)

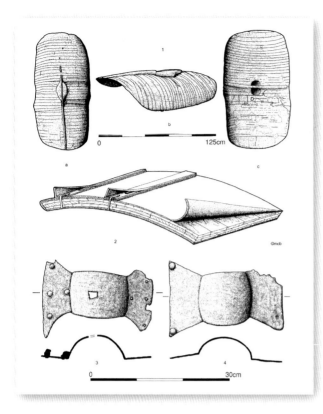

In battle each legionary carried a large oval shield (*scutum*) described by Polybius as being curved, 66cm wide, at least 1.1m long, and as 'thick as a palm'. It consisted of planks glued together rather like modern plywood, surrounded by an iron rim that could withstand blows on its edge, and with an iron boss running down its length, thicker in the middle, that could be used offensively to punch an opponent. (Courtesy M.C. Bishop)

generally tolerated for the goods and services they might provide. In an extreme crisis both *calones* and *lixae* would be expected to rally to the defence of the camp.

A commander would choose the site of a camp with great care, looking to augment the defences by exploiting natural features of the terrain and ensure access to wood, forage and water. A blind spot in the generalship of Antony was his lack of attention to such details. According to Vegetius, a camp 'must not be commanded by any higher ground' from where it could be observed by the enemy, 'nor must the location be liable to floods which would expose the army to great danger.' The exigencies of his strategic situation might mitigate somewhat the negative impression created by Antony deliberately breaking both of these rules. He was lucky during the Philippi campaign that his ignoring another basic tenet of camp site selection – namely that when an army is expected to be quartered for a protracted period it needs to be established on salubrious ground – did not have serious repercussions. Although he constructed his headquarters right next to a swamp the autumn weather negated the threat of malaria. During the Actium campaign his luck would run out.

By the terminal Republic period the old system by which legions would be raised on an ad hoc basis to meet a particular contingency and subsequently dissolved no longer applied. The legions had become institutionalized, evolving their own collegial identities based on geographic markers, such as Caesar's I Germanica and III Gallica, or boasts of martial prowess, such as Caesar's VI Ferrata ('Ironclad') and XII Fulminata ('Armed with Lightning').

A legion was composed of 60 centuries, each containing 80 soldiers. Six centuries formed a cohort; there were 10 cohorts per legion, each 480 men strong, meaning under optimal conditions a legion comprised 4,800 men. This establishment figure was seldom met in reality, especially after a protracted period in the field. One refinement to the template of the legion that emerged during the terminal Republic period was for the first cohort of each legion to be effectively doubled in size to 800 men, thereby adding more weight to the far right of the battle line.

Raising an army was the exclusive preserve of the senatorial elite as it required political appointment and substantial funds. Once ensconced with propraetorial or proconsular authority in the provinces, far beyond the oversight of Rome, a governor had virtual carte blanche to undertake military initiatives as he saw fit; blatant imperial aggrandizement could always be retrospectively justified to the Senate as pre-emptive defence against an imminent threat. Ambition, talent and success fed each other in a mutually reinforcing spiral of martial aggression as victories accrued loot and attracted recruits. At the conclusion of a particularly rewarding campaign an army would proclaim its commander *imperator*, an acclamation necessary for a general to apply to the Senate for a triumph.

Command of a legion under the authority of the general devolved upon the legate (*legati*); subordinate officers included the military tribunes (*tribuni militum*) and the prefect of the camp (*praefectus castrorum*), who was responsible for logistics and day-to-day operations.

The backbone of the army was Rome's junior officer class, the centurion. There were 59 of these men to a legion, five in the first cohort and six each in cohorts 2–10. Each cohort comprised six centuries, which retained the old manipular designations of *hastatus*, *princeps* and *pilus*, each divided between three maniples. In battle each century would be led by a centurion on the far right of the front line, a *tesserarius* (sergeant) stationed at the opposite end of the front line, and an *optio* (deputy) in the rear rank. A century also had a *signifer* (standard-bearer) and *cornicen* (trumpeter) attached. The former served as the visual marker for a rallying point while the latter functioned to relay basic strategic commands.

The senior centurion of a cohort, the *pilus prior*, may have had command of the entire cohort, but there is no evidence for this. The restrictions on command and control given the inherent limitations in communications technology under battlefield conditions may have rendered any prospect of centralized tactical direction moot; each centurion would be expected to respond to threats and opportunities on his own recognizance.

Personal identification was critical to unit cohesion; 'Lest the soldiers in the confusion of battle should be separated from their comrades,' Vegetius notes, each man's shield would bear a design, the *digmata*, advertising the owner's name, the number of his cohort, his century (by the centurion's name) and, in times of civil war, the name of his commander.

A legion had approximately 300 cavalry divided into ten squadrons of 30 horsemen attached to it, each squadron being commanded by a *decurio*. By Caesar's day most of Rome's cavalry needs were being met by *auxilia* from foreign nations, primarily Spaniards, Africans, Celts, and Germans. The same applied to light-armed and missile troops, Cretan archers and slingers from the Balearic Islands being popular choices. In another innovation of the terminal Republic period, the various warlords struggling for the succession in the wake of Caesar's death began to formally maintain permanent elite cohorts of troops dubbed praetorians (after the *praetorium*, the general's headquarters tent), the forebears of the imperial Praetorian Guard.

COMBAT

In a set-piece battle the clash of arms would commence when the commander displayed a flag, the *vexillum*, to signal the advance. The segmented nature of the legion allowed for a great deal of flexibility in its deployment allowing commanders to adjust to specific terrain and threat profiles to maximum effect. Typically, each legion would form up in three horizontal lines, the front line consisting of four cohorts, its centuries arranged ten wide by eight deep, the second and third lines of three cohorts each, their centuries arranged twelve wide by six deep.

This sketch of a military tribune named Minucius, from an original in Padua, depicts him in mufti, but with one hand kept warily on the hilt of his sword. (Courtesy Graham Sumner)

This carving depicts the fruits of Roman basic training; the legionary is crouched low behind the protection of his *scutum* and is poised to thrust upward with his *gladius* into the vitals of his enemy. (AAA Collection)

The intervals between the centuries were necessary to maintain cohesion and to prevent them dissolving into a disorganized mass. It was easier for an army to advance and maintain formation if this was carried out by small mobile units acting in unison rather than by a huge and unwieldy continuous line.

The definitive feature of the Roman method of warfare was the balance it struck between the individualized anarchy of the barbarian horde and the shoulder-to-shoulder rigidity of the Greek phalanx. A legionary's training emphasized individual initiative within the structural framework of his century, cohort and legion. A highly compact defensive formation of overlapping shields, the *testudo*, could be established for short periods in an emergency, but under combat conditions nothing was more important to the legionary than maintaining his defined personal space. Each legionary required 1.8m of frontage and it was vital that a commander not allow this space to be compromised because of pressure from front, flanks or rear crowding the centuries together, thereby dissolving unit structure. Under such a scenario, when the legionaries could no longer undertake offensive or defensive manoeuvres effectively because they were being crowded by their neighbours, compression panic would ensue.

So long as unit structure was maintained the legionary would think in terms of the collective interests of the unit. The more he sensed he was being herded into a contracting space by forces outside his control, the more the legionary would think only in terms of his own interests. His first instinct would be flight; if this was not possible, if the legionaries had been backed into a corner or encircled, a terrible slaughter would ensue as those men engaging the enemy would instinctively shrink back upon their comrades, further inhibiting their capacity to defend themselves. This resulted in disaster at Cannae in 216 BC and at the Bagradas River in 49 BC, in the latter instance the legionaries being so tightly packed together 'every corpse stood erect, crushed in a mass.' The genius of Caesar was displayed in his ability to recognize the initial stages of this process and incorporate an effective response whenever it arose. Caught off guard at the Sambre in 57 BC Caesar ordered the XII legion to open its formation so that the men could use their swords more effectively; trapped on an open plain at Ruspina in 46 BC he organized his force into two parallel lines back to back with enough space between them to rally and launch local counterattacks.

The front line of battle has been described by Sabin as being defined by the bonds of mutual deterrence. That is to say, the primary motivation of the fighting men on both sides is self-preservation. In most Roman battles the lines only sporadically come into contact, as one side or the other, or both, surged forwards for a brief and localized flurry of hand-to-hand combat that would end when one side got the worse of the exchange, its troops retreating to the default position while brandishing their weapons to deter immediate enemy pursuit. Roman sub-units such as centuries, maniples, and cohorts offered an ideal basis for such localized surges, which would typically be led by the junior officers and spearheaded by the veterans who best understood the rhythms of close-quarters combat. Appian, in his depiction of the battle of Forum Gallorum, noted of the veterans engaged that 'When they grew exhausted, they separated for a short breathing space, just as in gymnastic exercises, and then were locked together again. There was astonishment among the newcomers who had come up, seeing this going on with such discipline and in such silence.'

This kind of dynamic stand-off punctuated by episodes of hand-to-hand combat could continue for some time until one side finally lost its ability to resist, thereby breaking the bonds of mutual deterrence between the two sides and encouraging the opposing troops to surge forwards and begin killing in earnest. The most common mechanism for such a transformation would obviously be the panic of losing troops due to the breaching of their line, a psychological shock such as the death of the general, or the sheer accumulation of casualties and fatigue.

This model suggests how one side could gradually 'push' another back over distances of hundreds of yards, since if it was always the same side that gave way after the sporadic flurries of hand-to-hand combat, the accumulation of such small withdrawals would have significant grand tactical impact over time.

Command and control was problematic throughout antiquity given the technological limitations restricting the transfer of orders to visual markers – standards and flags – and trumpet signals. The ultimate rallying point for each legionary was the eagle standard (*aquila*) of the legion, which was imbued with semi-divine qualities. To bear it was a great honour; its loss was the ultimate disgrace. (Art Archive)

The real benefit of the multiple-line system can be appreciated in terms of the endurance and staying power of the entire legion that accrued from initially holding the supporting lines back out of missile range. Not only would front-rankers quickly become physically exhausted by the effort of even sporadic close combat, but all ranks would be subjected to intense and prolonged physical and emotional stress as they steeled themselves to surge forwards against an enemy just a few yards away, prepared themselves to counter a similar sudden charge by their adversaries at any moment, and kept a constant watch on the sky so as to be ready to intercept or dodge any incoming missiles.

The chain of command and control became extremely tenuous once the armies became locked together. With tens of thousands of men – not to mention horses – engaged in combat or on the march within a defined space the noise must have been terrific. Legionaries were encouraged to beat their shields with their *pila* as they advanced and utter a collective war cry as they closed to contact with the enemy. In the heat of battle under these conditions officers were forced to resort to shouts and hand-signals to convey orders.

Battles seldom took place during inclement weather (although the battle of Forum Gallorum took place on 'a day of hail', according to Ovid in the *Fasti*), but conversely, dry conditions meant the armies would often churn up vast clouds of dust. Dust would shape the outcome at Philippi, bringing the first battle to a premature close in a welter of confusion and misinformation.

Each legionary was expected to do three things well: march, fight and pitch camp. The latter task was standardized, enabling the construction of fortifications and living quarters according to a set format everywhere the legion served, allowing for rapid mobilization. This example, preserved in the desert at the foot of Masada, dates from more than a century after Philippi, but its basic contours would not be unfamiliar to servicemen from that era. (Author's collection)

POLITICS

To meet the insatiable demand for the raw material of war, recruiting agents (the *conquistores*) were hired to enlist male citizens (the *iuniores*) eligible for service, technically limited to those aged 17 to 46, though exceptions would be made at either end of the scale. The common soldier (*miles gregarious*) signed on for a 16-year term of service.

Brunt calculates that by the end of 43 BC the Triumvirs had 43 legions under their direct command, while the Republicans disposed of 21. Acknowledging the fact that approximately ten of these legions were vernacular, and incorporating those legions on garrison duty in Sardinia and Spain, and the rogue elements under Sextus, at this time some 216,000 to 270,000 Italians and 48,000 to 60,000 provincials were enlisted.

Figures by Scheidel note that the ratio of legionaries to *iuniores* by the end of 43 BC was 1:2.51, a proportion not realized since the darkest days of the struggle with Hannibal during the Second Punic War. Put another way, as the conflict over the dying Republic reached its climax the ratio of legionaries to citizens was 1:11.6, meaning more than one of every 12 adult Roman males was in uniform.

As the tide of war ebbed and flowed during the terminal phase of the Republic new legions were constantly being formed around a cadre of re-enlisted veterans; in the wake of the Mutina campaign demobilized Caesarean veterans were reorganized into rival VII and VIII legions under the command of Antony and Octavian. Recruitment of these *evocati* – veterans who had completed the standard term of service but chose to re-enlist – was made easier by their tendency to cluster in defined locales. These communities, identified as *collegia*, were maintained along military lines with their inhabitants referring to each other as *fraters*, making the transition back into active service a relatively smooth one.

Another repercussion of the incessant demand on manpower during the terminal Republic was the evaporation of the taboo against the formation of legions comprised of non-Italians (*peregrini*). Caesar had enrolled a vernacular legion, the V *Alauda* ('Larks'), while serving in Gaul, and during the 40s we hear of a number of vernacular legions being raised in Spain, Macedonia and the East.

But the most distinctive trait of the legions of this era was their unprecedented political self-identity. During the brief period of transition between the Republican and imperial forms of government the veterans demanded consideration of their rights and entitlements and on numerous occasions acted independently to impose their will on the men who ostensibly commanded them. These stirrings of democracy in the ranks had manifested themselves during the Civil War when even the legendary Caesar had struggled to subdue two mutinies and had completely lost control of his legions at Thapsus, who slaughtered their enemy after they had surrendered and even, 'mad with rage and bitter resentment', wounded or killed those of their own officers who attempted to intervene. They reached their apogee in the extraordinary spectacle of the *senatus caligatus*, a military tribunal mockingly named after the soldier's footwear, offering to arbitrate the conflict between Octavian and Antony's brother and wife in 41 BC and, when that failed, the legions mediating the resolution of the subsequent stand-off between Antony and Octavian at Brundisium the following year.

The opportunity for plunder while in the service and a donative of land upon retirement were the inducements for enlistment during this protracted period of civil war. According to Botermann, the desire to avenge Caesar's death was not an overriding priority for most legions commanded by the Triumvirs except those composed of the veterans who had served directly under him, especially the centurions. Of Lepidus's seven legions, two were composed of *evocati*, four of veterans, and one uncertain; of Antony's 11, three were composed of *evocati*, five of veterans, two of recruits, and one uncertain; and of Octavian's 17, two were composed of *evocati*, four of veterans, while no fewer than 11 of the legions that elected to serve with the heir to Caesar were made up of recruits who had never served with his adoptive father.

Political loyalties were fluid in the terminal Republic, and this had a commensurate impact on military discipline. Desertion, once a capital offence, was now actually rewarded, and whole armies resorted to it. In this mercenary environment the legions were solely self-interested and motivated by the desire for security, which for the vast majority meant land of their own. For this reason, in the wake of Philippi, Ferrero writes, 'if the Triumvirs were the masters of the empire, they were also the slaves of the legions.' Aware that political authority rested not in ballots but in swords, Appian describes the rank and file as 'contemptuous of their rulers in the knowledge that they needed them to confirm their power.'

FROM MUTINA TO THE
SECOND TRIUMVIRATE

In early March Hirtius and Octavian advanced on Mutina. En route, they took possession of Bononia, which had been abandoned by its garrison, and routed the cavalry which later confronted them, leaving only Pollentia (Pollenzo) and Regium Lepidi in Antony's hands. But Antony had learned enough under Caesar at Alesia to know how a Roman officer should conduct a siege. In addition to inner lines of circumvallation encircling Mutina he had established outer lines of contravallation to block any attempt at relief of the town. The senatorial leaders attempted to signal their presence to Decimus by lighting beacon signals from the tallest trees. When this failed they scratched a few words on a thin sheet of lead which they rolled up like paper and gave to a courier, who swam with it across the River Scultenna by night. Decimus replied in like fashion, establishing a viable, if tenuous, communications link.

With its winter stores nearly exhausted, famine was beginning to gnaw at the garrison trapped in Mutina, but Hirtius and Octavian were determined to wait for Pansa to arrive with reinforcements before confronting Antony. There were frequent cavalry engagements, as Antony had a much larger force of horse, but the marshy ground deprived him of the chance to take full

'Friends, Romans, countrymen, lend me your ears!' Shakespeare's rendition of Antony's funeral address brilliantly interprets the rhetoric that turned popular opinion against the assassins and, briefly, made Antony first man in Rome. (Bridgeman)

advantage of this superiority. More significantly, when some foraging parties on both sides came to blows, drawing in additional contingents from both sides, a sharp battle ensued in which Antony was victorious.

On 19 March Pansa set out to link up with Hirtius and Octavian, bringing four legions of recruits, having left one, the *legio urbana*, to defend Rome. Antony was aware his best chance of breaking the senatorial relief effort was to prevent it from being consolidated. On 14 April, after leaving orders for the bulk of his army to continue provoking the enemy and thus make it appear, as far as possible, that he himself was still present, Antony marched with his praetorian cohort, the II and the XXXV legions, light-armed troops and a strong body of cavalry to cut off Pansa before he could reach the senatorial armies. Antony assumed Pansa had only four legions of recruits, but the previous night Hirtius had dispatched the tribune Decimus Carfulenus with the Martian legion and Octavian's praetorian cohort to assist him in completing the last stage of the Via Aemilia as it passed through a narrow defile.

We have two accounts of the ensuing battle. Unfortunately, they differ in almost every detail. In a letter to Cicero, Sulpicius Galba – a legate of Caesar's during the Gallic campaign who had sided with the Senate and was serving with the Martians – described how Antony stationed the bulk of his men under cover at the village of Forum Gallorum (Castelfranco Emilia), en route to Mutina along the Via Aemilia. The battle opened when Antony's cavalry and light-armed troops went on ahead and succeeded in drawing the Martian legion and Pansa's cavalry in pursuit. Pansa ordered two legions of recruits to advance after them while he remained in camp with the remaining two legions and the baggage train.

On approaching Forum Gallorum the Martians drew up in a line consisting of 12 cohorts. At that point Antony sprang his trap. On the Via Aemilia itself the Senatorial left wing, consisting of only two cohorts of the Martian legion and two praetorian cohorts, was forced to give ground, because it was in danger of being outflanked by Antony's cavalry, but on the Senatorial right wing, eight cohorts of the Martian legion under the command of Sulpicius Galba put Antony's XXXV legion to flight, advancing more than 500 paces beyond their original line. The retreat of the XXXV legion may have been staged in order to lure the Martians into a trap. According to

The Pons Fabricius, constructed in 62 BC. The oldest extant bridge in Rome, it spans half of the Tiber River, from the Campus Martius on the east side to Tiber Island in the middle. Lepidus would have brought the troops he had stationed on Tiber Island into the city across this bridge in the confused aftermath of the ides of March. (Felix Just, S.J.)

The Battle of Forum Gallorum, according to Galba's account, 14 April 43 BC

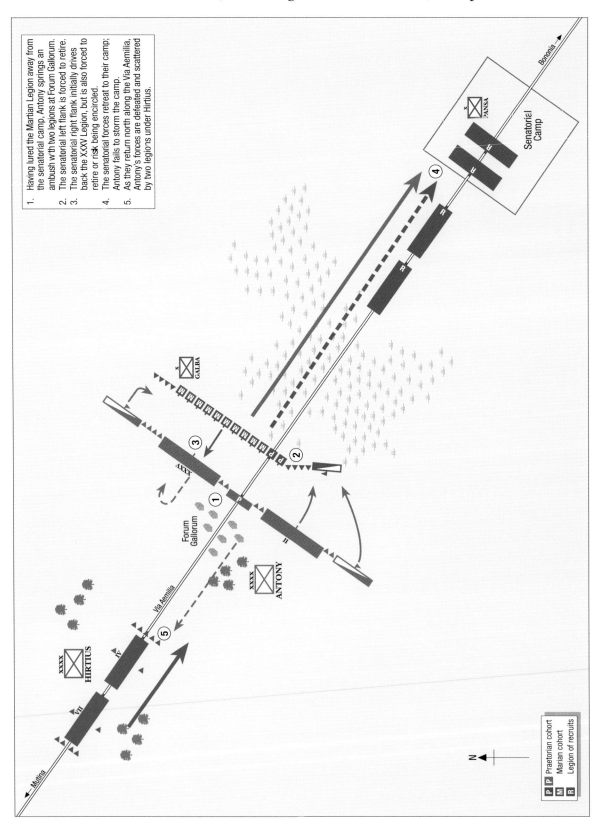

1. Having lured the Martian Legion away from the senatorial camp, Antony springs an ambush with two legions at Forum Gallorum.
2. The senatorial left flank is forced to retire.
3. The senatorial right flank initially drives back the XXXV Legion, but is also forced to retire or risk being encircled.
4. The senatorial forces retreat to their camp; Antony fails to storm the camp.
5. As they return north along the Via Aemilia, Antony's forces are defeated and scattered by two legions under Hirtius.

PANSA

GALBA

XXXV

Forum Gallorum

Via Aemilia

ANTONY

II

HIRTIUS

V

VII

Senatorial Camp

Bononia

Mutina

N

P P	Praetorian cohort
M	Marian cohort
R	Legion of recruits

The Battle of Forum Gallorum, according to Appian's account, 14 April 43 BC

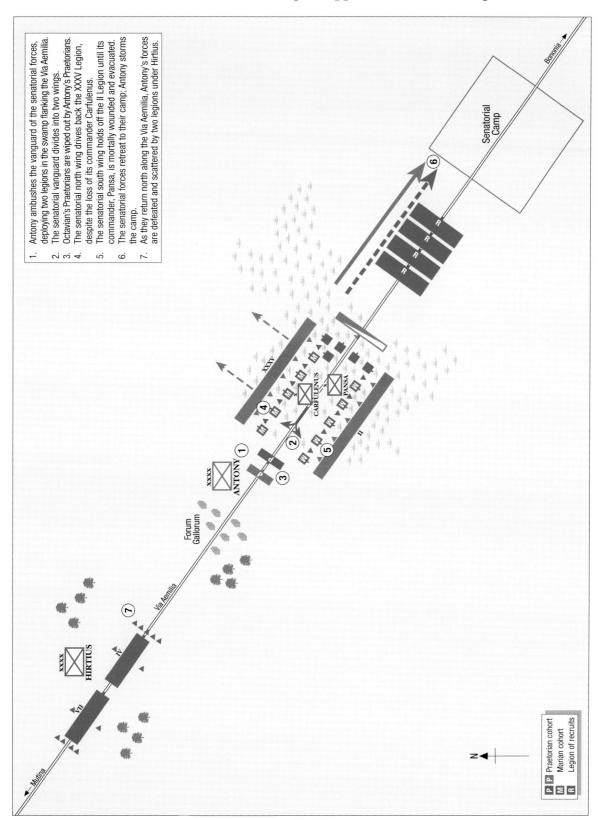

1. Antony ambushes the vanguard of the senatorial forces, deploying two legions in the swamp flanking the Via Aemilia.
2. The senatorial vanguard divides into two wings.
3. Octavian's Praetorians are wiped out by Antony's Praetorians.
4. The senatorial north wing drives back the XXXV Legion, despite the loss of its commander Carfulenus.
5. The senatorial south wing holds off the II Legion until its commander, Pansa, is mortally wounded and evacuated.
6. The senatorial forces retreat to their camp; Antony storms the camp.
7. As they return north along the Via Aemilia, Antony's forces are defeated and scattered by two legions under Hirtius.

Senatorial Camp

Bononia

XXXV

CARFULENUS

PANSA

II

ANTONY
XXXX

Forum Gallorum

Via Aemilia

HIRTIUS
XXXX

IV

VII

Mutina

N

P P Praetorian cohort
M Marian cohort
R Legion of recruits

ABOVE LEFT
Dating from c. 120 BC, the Temple of Hercules Victor, located in the Forum Boarium, is the earliest surviving marble building in Rome.

ABOVE RIGHT
The Temple of Portunus, dating from c. 100 BC, also stood in the Forum Boarium, the oldest forum constructed in Rome, lying between the Capitoline, the Palatine and Aventine hills. The Forum Boarium was adjacent to the Port Tibernius, the main port of Rome.

Galba, 'when the cavalry attempted to outflank our wing, I began to retire and to throw my light-armed troops in the way of the Moorish cavalry, to prevent their charging my men in the rear.' Conscious that he was now in danger of being encircled, Galba rode hard, 'with my shield slung behind my back', to contact the legions of recruits that were on their way up from the Senatorial camp. 'Antony's men set off in pursuit of me,' he reported to Cicero, 'while our own men began pouring in a volley of *pila*.' Fortunately, Galba survived this exposure to friendly fire and was able to link up the Senatorial forces, which withdrew in good order to their camp.

Antony attempted to follow up his tactical success by storming the Senatorial camp but this action was a costly failure. Worse was to follow; as Antony withdrew he was attacked by Hirtius with 20 veteran cohorts, who destroyed or put to flight his whole force, taking two eagles and 60 standards. Antony, with his cavalry, straggled back to his camp near Mutina after sunset.

In the account of the historian Appian, Antony placed his two best legions in ambush in a marsh, where they were concealed by the reeds and where the road, which had been thrown up artificially, was narrow. Pansa and Carfulenus had hurried ahead through the defile by night. At daybreak, with only the Martian legion and five other cohorts, they entered the marsh, 'where there was a suspicious agitation of the rushes, then a gleam here and there of shield and helmet.' When Antony's praetorian cohort blocked the road it was the signal for the rest of his forces to attack the Senatorial troops on their flanks.

The Martian legion, surrounded on all sides and having no way to escape, ordered the new levies, if they came up, not to join in the fight lest they should cause confusion by their inexperience. The praetorians of Octavian confronted the praetorians of Antony. The other cohorts split and advanced into the marsh on either side, one flank commanded by Pansa, the other by Carfulenus. Thus there were two battles in the marsh, and neither division could see the other by reason of the elevated road, while along the road itself the praetorian cohorts fought another battle of their own.

The praetorians of Octavian perished to the last man. Carfulenus was killed in action but his Martians got the better of those opposed to them, who gave way; those under Pansa held out until Pansa was wounded in the side by a javelin and carried off the field to Bononia. Then his soldiers retired, at first step by step, but then in flight. When the new levies saw this they fled in disorder to their camp, but the Martians formed up to make a last stand outside it. Antony refrained from attacking these veteran troops, 'but he fell upon the new levies and made a great slaughter.'

When word of the ambush reached Hirtius in camp 11km away he immediately marched to the rescue with the IV and VII legions. By the time he made contact with the enemy it 'was already evening and the victorious Antonians were returning singing hymns of triumph.' The tables had turned for Antony; now it was his men who were tired, outnumbered, and caught on the march. Hirtius won a decisive victory, but chose not to pursue the beaten remnant into both the swamp and the gathering darkness. Antony's cavalry went to the assistance of the wounded and those who had found refuge in the marsh and collected them through the night. Antony and Pansa each lost about half of their men, Octavian's praetorian cohort being wiped out; Hirtius's losses were slight. The next day both sides withdrew to their respective camps outside Mutina.

These accounts can only be harmonized in their broadest outline; Antony sought to liquidate Pansa before he could link up with the senatorial armies; after an initial success he was in turn surprised and defeated by Hirtius. Hirtius was saluted as *imperator* by his soldiers and by the Senate (as were Pansa, although he had fared badly, and Octavian, although he had not even been engaged). In a further boost to senatorial morale, Pontius Aquila, a legate of Decimus, defeated Munatius Plancus and drove him out of Pollentia.

It is clear Antony now felt the initiative slipping away and at risk of being reduced from besieger to besieged. In the wake of the setback at Forum Gallorum he decided against seeking another general engagement with the Senatorial armies but sought to keep them at bay by harassing them daily with his cavalry until Decimus was finally starved into surrender. For this very reason Hirtius and Octavian were determined to provoke a fight.

Further complicating the picture, a force dispatched by Lepidus arrived in the theatre. Although ostensibly acting on behalf of the Senate, Lepidus, hedging his bets, had given no clear instructions to his legate, Marcus Silanus, regarding which of the two sides he was sending the army. Silanus, doubtless knowing his superior's true motives, went on his own recognizance to Antony.

According to the veteran orator and statesman Marcus Tullius Cicero, the assassins of Caesar acted with 'no plan, no thought, no method'. Cicero negotiated the political compromise that stabilized the tottering Republic. The respite was brief, however; less than two months after the ides of March, Cicero was already writing to Cassius that 'it appears we are free of the despot, but not of the despotism.' (Bildarchiv Preussischer Kulturbesitz/Art Resource, NY)

This structure in the forum is all that remains of the mausoleum where Caesar's ashes were interred. His corpse was immolated on this spot by the plebs of Rome, who gave vent to their grief by spontaneously erecting a funeral pyre and feeding the flames with their personal effects; veteran soldiers cast their arms and armour into the blaze; women added their jewellery. (Felix Just, S.J.)

As Antony still would not come out when Hirtius and Octavian offered battle, on 21 April they moved towards the far side of Mutina where it was less closely besieged on account of the rough ground, as if about to force their way into the town. Suspecting a bluff, Antony was initially content to shadow this manoeuvre with his cavalry, but he then either sensed an opportunity or lost his nerve and brought up two legions from his camp, giving his enemies the battle they were looking for. Antony ordered up other legions from other camps, but because they came up slowly, or they were caught off guard, or because of the distances involved or poor coordination with the reinforcements under Silanus, his army was overwhelmed. But it would prove to be a costly victory for the Senate; Hirtius broke into Antony's camp before being killed, fighting near Antony's tent; Aquila fell in the same battle. Octavian held the enemy's camp until he was driven out by Antony. Both sides passed the night under arms. Against the advice of his officers, who urged him to continue the siege, Antony the following day resolved to withdraw his army (the still intact V and the remnants of II and XXXV legions, and more than 5,000 cavalry) in a bid to link up with Ventidius and his three legions from Picenum (the VII, VIII and IX), and seek support from Lepidus and Plancus.

When news of the victory reached Rome a crowd of citizens spontaneously bore Cicero through the streets from his house to the Senate. It was the pinnacle of his career; with Antony on the run the Senate finally declared him a *hostis*, an enemy of the state. The forces of legitimacy appeared to be triumphant, but the reality in the field was quite different.

Antony had been able to secure a two-day head start over the Senatorial coalition, for Decimus, only now made aware of the death of Hirtius, immediately went to Bononia to consult with Pansa only to find that the consul too had succumbed to his wounds. It was the first time both consuls had been killed in action since 208 BC. The crisis of legitimacy this created became immediately apparent when Decimus urged Octavian to march south and cut off Ventidius before he could link up with Antony. Octavian not only snubbed the assassin of his adopted father but refused to hand over Pansa's legions. It is uncertain if the rank and file would have accepted Senatorial authority even if Octavian had been prepared to submit to it.

The Senate, prematurely assuming the crisis had passed, overplayed its hand. To complement an unprecedented 50-day period of thanksgiving for the victory at Mutina, it voted a triumph for Decimus, but refused even an ovation to Octavian. It also decreed that authority for the prosecution of the war and the two dead consuls' legions should be transferred to Decimus's command. Finally, it reduced the bounties promised to Octavian's troops and stalled on the plan for distributing the land they had been promised, establishing a commission – that did not include Octavian – to determine the terms of the settlement.

The Senate further alienated the heir of Caesar by legitimizing the acquisitions of Brutus and Cassius in the east and voting supreme naval command to Sextus Pompey, who had advanced to Massilia (Marseilles). It appeared to Octavian that the Senate was determined to marginalize him. He began to plan accordingly.

Antony, meanwhile, marched west to Parma (which was ransacked) and Placentia and then by the Via Milvia to Dertona, picking up – or forcefully recruiting – citizens and slaves along the way, before turning south and crossing the Ligurian Alps to arrive at Vada Sabatia, 50km south-west of Genoa. Here

on 3 May he was reunited with Ventidius, who, with the established routes in the hands of the Senate, had been forced to undertake an equally hazardous forced march over the Apennines. Decimus struggled to keep pace with, let alone overtake, his quarry; he wrote in extenuation to Cicero that his 'apology of an army,' which had barely recovered from the privations of the siege at Mutina, had no pack animals, no horses, and little money with which to continue the pursuit. He was also uncertain whether Antony's intention was to seek out Lepidus, keep to the mountains and use his cavalry to fight a guerrilla war, or double back into the now undefended Etruria.

In the event Antony feinted north with his cavalry under Trebellius towards Pollentia. Decimus fell for the ruse, immediately sending five cohorts in advance and following up with his whole army moving westwards; he later expressed 'no small satisfaction' to Cicero at having occupied Pollentia an hour ahead of Trebellius, but this shadow-boxing had merely enabled Antony to enter Gallia Narbonensis unmolested. He marched to Forum Julii towards the middle of the month and made camp less than 40km from Lepidus who was at Forum Voconii.

Fatally for the Senate, the provincial governors and their legions outside Italy had never been more than ostensibly under its command. Lepidus in Gallia Narbonensis and Hispania Citerior, Munatius Plancus in Gallia Comata, and Asinius Pollio in Hispania Ulterior had been raising fresh troops and recalling veterans in the expectation of fresh fighting. Lepidus had been able to re-form Caesar's old VI from its colony at Arelate, and X from Narbo. All three remained in contact with Rome, vigorously asserting their loyalty to the Senatorial cause while not doing anything to advance it. On 29 April Decimus had urged Cicero to extract a commitment from 'that arrant weathercock Lepidus, so that he does not let Antony join him, and perhaps make us fight the war all over again.'

Its numerous anachronisms notwithstanding, *Les massacres du Triumvirat*, painted by Antoine Caron in 1566, offers a glimpse into the surreal perversion of Rome during the proscriptions, when legalized murder ruled the streets. (Art Archive)

Caesar's appointment of Marcus Lepidus as his Master of the Horse was a reflection of the value the dictator placed on his administrative skills, not his command abilities in the field. Lepidus would be marginalized by his colleagues in the Triumvirate and fade into the background of history as Shakespeare's 'slight and unmeritable man.' (Andreas Pangerl, www.romancoins.info)

Lepidus allowed the fraternization between his army and that of Antony to serve as the harbinger for the reconciliation of the two commanders. He pleaded innocence to the Senate, lamenting that 'Fortune wrenched my decision away from me,' his army having mutinied, 'and, to tell the truth, has forced me to champion the lives and safety of so vast a number of Roman citizens.'

Anticipating this outcome, Cicero wrote to Plancus on 5 May, reminding him 'all our hopes are pinned on you' and urging him to ensure 'not a spark of this abominable war is left alive.' Plancus had made camp at Cularo (Grenoble) where Decimus joined him towards the end of June. Their combined armies were imposing on paper, totalling 14 legions, but only four of these were veterans.

The Senatorial position utterly collapsed when Pollio went over to Antony, bringing with him two legions and, more importantly, the opening to reconciliation with Plancus. Decimus had no option but to withdraw in a bid to link up with Brutus via Illyricum. Deserted little by little by his army, he was finally finished off by one of Antony's agents in the house of a Celtic chieftan with whom he had taken refuge.

Antony was now master of all Spain and Gaul. The only obstacle between him and Rome was Octavian, still at Bononia, and the Senate's last champion was determined to extract every concession this pre-eminence entitled him to.

In the middle of May an anxious Brutus wrote to Cicero from Macedonia to express his alarm about reports Octavian was seeking one of the vacant consulships. His fear would be swiftly realized. Under the constitution the minimum age for election to the office of consul was 41 years of age for patricians, 42 for plebeians, and Octavian was still in his teens. In early July he dispatched an envoy of centurions to petition the Senate for an exemption to this threshold. When it was refused Octavian promptly led eight legions across the Rubicon in a march on Rome. In thus emulating his father Octavian had chosen the path of force over law and the Republic had lost its last succour in the West.

The Senate panicked at his approach, offering Octavian the right to stand for consul *in absentia* and his men their promised full 5,000 denarii bonus. At that moment two legions arrived from Africa, bringing the total under the control of the Senate to three. The Senate promptly rescinded its offer. Undaunted, Octavian camped outside Rome and marched into the forum the following day escorted by only his praetorians. The city's three legions came over to him. That night, seizing on a rumour the IV and Martian legions had mutinied, Cicero tried to galvanize resistance, but the rumour proved false, and the orator fled Rome.

Octavian ordered a donative of 2,500 denarii to each legionary from the public funds, with the balance to be paid later. After taking office as consul on 22 September, the day before his 20th birthday, he prevailed upon his colleague in the office to pass the *lex Pedia*, a law establishing the murder of Caesar as a capital crime. He then left for the reckoning with Antony.

Octavian's march on Rome secured him the three legions there (the two from Africa and the *legio urbana*) bringing his total to 11. He gained six more when the three legions raised by Pansa and the three raised by Decimus came over to his side.

Ironically, the four legions that had served under Decimus at Mutina passed under the control of Antony, bringing his total to eight. In alliance with the seven led by Lepidus, the three Plancus had available, and the two Pollio could spare, Antony could now put 20 legions in the field (and 10,000 cavalry) against the 17 commanded by Octavian, nominally in the name of the Senate.

In reality, Octavian was seeking terms, not battle. As a gesture of good faith, he had ordered the decrees of outlawry levied against Antony and Lepidus be revoked. In full view of their armies, and having frisked each other for concealed weapons, the three men met in a conference on a small island in a river near Bononia. The negotiations culminated in the *tresviri rei publicae constituendae*, the Second Triumvirate, its members assuming unlimited power for a five-year term to restore order to the Roman state. To cement their reconciliation Octavian agreed to marry Clodia, a daughter of Antony's wife Fulvia by her former husband Clodius.

Under the terms of their pact, Antony, with 16 legions, was to govern Gallia Cisalpina and Gallia Comata; Lepidus, with 10 legions, Gallia Narbonensis and the two Spains; Octavian, with 17 legions, Africa and the islands of the western Mediterranean; Italy would remain common ground. In the event, Lepidus lent three of his legions to Octavian and four to Antony, bringing both to a full complement of 20 as the war against Brutus and Cassius commenced. Lepidus stayed in Rome to uphold the interests of the Triumvirate with his three remaining legions.

The Triumvirs had power; they lacked money and the submission of the political elite. In a bid to secure both simultaneously, on 27 November they introduced successive bills of proscription, empowering them to take the lives and assets of hundreds of senators and thousands of equestrians. Among the victims were Cicero and his brother Quintus, who made a bid to reach the coast at Astura and take ship to join Brutus in Macedonia. Quintus was killed en route. Cicero was run to ground at his villa at Caieta, near Formiae, by a party led by a military tribune, Popilius Laenas, whom Cicero had once defended in a civil case. His head and hands were presented to Antony, who had them nailed to the rostrum in the Forum, but not before his wife Fulvia had seized the opportunity to open the famed orator's mouth and pierce his tongue with her hairpin.

Almost unnoticed in the wake of Caesar's death, Cleopatra slipped out of Rome and returned to Egypt. Her priority was maintaining the independence of her kingdom; her trump card was her son by Caesar, Caesarion, depicted nursing at her breast in this coin. (American Numismatic Society)

THE ROAD TO PHILIPPI

BRUTUS'S MOVEMENTS

Brutus had arrived in Athens in the autumn of 44 BC and soon attracted an entourage of admiring young students, including Marcus Cicero, the son of the orator. However, his agenda extended far beyond attending performances of philosophical rhetoric. To lay the foundations for an independent military command he first needed money. Brutus intercepted the annual tribute Trebonius was sending from Asia to Rome in Euboea and persuaded the official in charge to hand it over. The quaestors of Asia and Syria – Marcus Appuleius and Antistius Vetus – supplied him with additional funds.

With money under his command Brutus was now in a position to command men. In a major coup the last of the Macedonian legions which Lucius Piso, the lieutenant of Antony, commanded surrendered itself to Marcus Cicero. Dolabella's cavalry, on the march to Syria in two divisions, in Thessaly and Macedonia, also declared for Brutus. With this force Brutus advanced to Thessalonica where the lame duck governor of Macedonia, Hortensius Hortalus, willingly hailed Brutus as his successor. Brutus then dispatched an expedition to Demetrias, where it seized the great quantity of arms stockpiled for the abortive Parthian war.

The Acropolis, rising above the Agora in Athens. The nucleus of the Republican army-in-exile rallied around Brutus after his arrival here in the autumn of 44 BC. (Author's collection)

In early January, after news reached Thessalonica Gaius Antonius had arrived in Macedonia to succeed Hortensius, Brutus immediately set out on a forced march to the Adriatic. Gaius had the support of Publius Vatinius, the governor of Illyricum, who seized Dyrrachium before Brutus could stop him. But Vatinius had lost the confidence of his men. A revolt had broken out in Illyricum upon the death of Caesar. Vatinius had lost five cohorts in an ambush and his army was unpaid. The three legions under his command promptly deserted to Brutus.

Gaius, with only one legion, tried to level the odds by setting an ambush for Brutus, but he escaped the trap and set an ambush in his turn. Brutus did no harm to those whom he caught, but ordered his soldiers to salute their adversaries and let them pass out of the trap unharmed. By a forced march via an alternate route he caught them again as they retreated, but again did them no harm, only paying them his respects by offering another salute. This time three cohorts of Gaius's men, thoroughly cowed, returned the salute and passed over to Brutus. Gaius fled to Apollonia with the remaining seven cohorts, where he was taken alive after being betrayed, the defenders throwing open the gates to receive Brutus.

Gaius plotted his revenge while in captivity by intriguing among the legions and stirring up a revolt. Brutus was able to prevent Gaius being rescued by putting him in a covered litter and, on the pretence that he was evacuating an invalid, smuggling him out of Apollonia. The disaffected soldiers, unable to find Gaius, seized a hill commanding the city. Brutus induced them to come to an understanding and hand over the instigators, of whom he executed some and dismissed others from his service. According to Dio, the rank and file were so eager to ingratiate themselves with Brutus they turned over all of Gaius's lieutenants and would have slaughtered them had he not put them aboard ships, as if he were going to drown them, and so conveyed them to safety.

Still uncertain of the mood of his men, Brutus entrusted Gaius Antonius to the care of Gaius Clodius and left him in Apollonia. He took the bulk of his army and retired into upper Macedonia and then sailed to Asia. Among the various allies whom he gained at this time was Deiotarus, the tetrarch of Galatia, who had refused his assistance to Cassius.

ABOVE
Gaius Antonius issued these coins, featuring the distinctive native cloak (*chlamys*) and cap (*kausia*), in celebration of being appointed Governor of Macedonia. The celebration would be brief; for the second time in a decade he would be captured by Republican forces on the eastern shore of the Adriatic. (Wayne Sayles)

ABOVE LEFT
The entrance to the ancient harbour (Mandraki) at Rhodes today is guarded by the Fortress of St Nicholas. Originally a tower constructed in 1464–67 by Grand Master Zacosta of the Knights of St John, the tower was turned into a small fortress by Grand Master d'Aubusson, who built a bastion around it after the first siege of Rhodes by the Ottoman Turks in 1480. (Author's collection)

Spooked by a rescue attempt launched by Mark Antony in a bid to free his brother, Clodius had Gaius executed; Brutus had originally wanted him kept alive but, after learning that Decimus had perished, washed his hands of his prisoner's fate. Brutus returned to Europe and campaigned in Thrace, winning over some clans and fighting others, winning enough success to be hailed as imperator before he withdrew again into Asia.

CASSIUS'S MOVEMENTS

The Colossus of Rhodes, one of the original seven wonders of the world, stood at the mouth of the city-state's harbour, but did not straddle it as imagined in this 16th-century engraving by Martin Heemskerck.

Cassius sailed from Italy to Smyrna, where he secured enough funds from Trebonius, the proconsul of Asia, to suborn many of the cavalry which Dolabella had sent in advance into Syria and recruit Asian and Cilician auxiliaries and a number of Parthian mounted archers, who were attracted by the reputation he had acquired among them in the aftermath of the debacle at Carrhae. Cassius advanced into Syria, intent on resolving the protracted siege of Apamea by bringing both sides under his banner. The legions of Murcus and Crispus immediately went over to him, as did that of Bassus, much to his *chagrin*; as Cassius remarked in a letter to Cicero on 7 May, Bassus, 'was sorely reluctant to hand over his legion to me, and if the troops had not sent me their representative against his will, he would have shut the gates and held Apamea until it was taken by storm.' Murcus and Crispus willingly accepted commands under Cassius; Bassus was dismissed unharmed.

Now with eight legions under his command Cassius marched into Judea where he intercepted the four legions Dolabella's legate Allienus was bringing up from Egypt. After accepting their surrender Cassius, virtually without a fight, had become the master of 12 legions and all of Rome's provinces in the East, from which he extorted an enormous war chest. Cassius exacted 700 talents of silver from Judea; towns that resisted, such as Gophna and Emmaus, were sold into slavery.

The first challenge to Cassius's authority in the east would come from Cicero's son-in-law. Dolabella had left Rome before the year of his consulship had concluded. But he did not immediately proceed to Syria; in need of funds he marched through Greece, Macedonia, Thrace, and Asia Minor, collecting and extorting as much as he could on his way before arriving at Smyrna in February 43 BC. When Trebonius did not admit Dolabella into the city Dolabella staged a march towards Ephesus before doubling back, entering Smyrna by night, executing Trebonius, and hurling his head at the feet of Caesar's statue; his soldiers later kicked it about the streets like a football. When news of this action reached Rome the Senate, aroused by the denunciation of Cicero, declared Dolabella a *hostis*.

Unfazed, Dolabella recruited a naval force from Rhodes, Lycia, Pamphylia, and Cilicia. He marched into Cilicia with two legions while Cassius was in Palestine, won over the people of Tarsus, brushed aside a detachment Cassius had left at Aegae, and invaded Syria. Failing to force his way into Antioch he fell back on Laodicea, a city built on a peninsula into the Mediterranean that allowed for close support by his fleet. Cassius defeated him in open battle and, having set up camp about 32km away at Paltus with 10 legions, 20 auxiliary cohorts and 4,000 horse, laid siege to Laodicea erecting a barricade across the isthmus 370m in length, composed of stones and all sorts of material assembled from suburban houses and tombs. Simultaneously, he sent to Rhodes and the cities of Phoenicia and Lycia for ships to prevent Dolabella from escaping by sea.

Despite only the city of Sidon responding to his appeal, Cassius fought a naval engagement with the vessels at hand. A number of ships were sunk on both sides and Dolabella captured five with their crews. Cassius again sent to those who had rejected his summons, and also to Cleopatra and to Serapio, her viceroy in Cyprus. The Tyrians, the Aradii and Serapio, not waiting to consult Cleopatra, sent Cassius what ships they had. The queen excused herself on the grounds that Egypt was at that time suffering from famine and pestilence, but she was really cooperating with Dolabella out of loyalty to the memory of Caesar. Rhodes and the Lycians re-emphasized their neutrality.

While Republican fleets under Cassius Parmensis, Lentulus Spinther and Tillius Cimber harried Dolabella it was Murcus who finally broke through into the harbour of Laodicea and overwhelmed Dolabella's fleet, cutting off his only means of flight. Once Cassius, through bribery, had penetrated the walls, Dolabella ordered one of his soldiers to kill him. His two legions were sworn into service under Cassius, who, according to Appian, 'plundered the temples and the treasury of Laodicea, punished the chief citizens, and exacted very heavy contributions from the rest, so that the city was reduced to extremest misery.'

Cassius next set his sights on Egypt, the richest of all Rome's client states, now virtually defenceless. Fortunately for Cleopatra, at this moment a message arrived from Brutus urging his colleague to link up with him at the earliest possible opportunity. Reluctantly, Cassius turned north, leaving his nephew to hold Syria with one legion. He also dismissed his Parthian volunteers with presents, sending ambassadors to their king to request a larger force of auxiliaries.

While this was going on the people of Tarsus had sought to prevent the governor of Bithynia, Tillius Cimber, an assassin of Caesar, from passing through the Taurus Mountains in order to link up with Cassius. Assuming he headed a powerful force they initially surrendered the pass and offered a truce,

THE FALL OF XANTHUS (pp. 42–43)

Brutus took personal command of the siege of Xanthus, the climax of his campaign in Lycia in early 42 BC. After destroying their suburbs the Xanthians withdrew into their heavily fortified city. Brutus divided his army into day and night rotations and maintained a round-the-clock siege, deploying battering-rams against the walls and launching assaults against the gates. In response to the constant pressure, the Xanthians, sensing a lull in the action, launched a night-time sortie only to fall into a trap. Those survivors who fled back to the gate they had issued from found it closed and were slaughtered under the walls.

The bitterly contested struggle nearly culminated in disaster for Brutus when a second sortie by the defenders succeeded in torching his siege engines. As the Xanthians withdrew approximately 2,000 Roman troops this time forced the gate in pursuit and broke into the city, but when the portcullis fell those legionaries who had avoided being crushed found their retreat cut off. Pelted by missiles hurled from the roofs in the narrow streets they fought their way into the forum and made a stand by the temple of Sarpedon. Their comrades outside, unable to break the portcullis or clear the ramparts because their rams and towers were in flames, fought desperately to rescue them. Some extemporized ladders by pushing the trunks of trees against the wall **(1)**, while others fastened iron hooks to ropes, hurled them over the battlements, and clambered up the vertical ascent **(2)**. Those who succeeded in scaling the wall opened a small gate, defended with a very dense palisade, admitting the most daring of the assailants, who swung themselves over the palings and joined in hacking at the portcullis on its undefended inner side until it finally gave way **(3)**. As night fell the Roman army streamed into the city, which the defenders torched rather than surrender. Only a handful of the inhabitants survived to see the next morning.

but once they perceived the small number of troops under his command they neither received him into their city nor furnished him with provisions. When he constructed a fort to secure his rear before setting out for Syria, believing it to be of more importance to aid Cassius than to destroy their city himself, they took possession of it and then set out to seize the rival city of Adana on the justification it was supporting Cassius. When Cassius heard of this he sent Lucius Rufus against Tarsus but came himself after eliminating Dolabella. Finding the city had already surrendered to Rufus without a struggle he chose to make an example of it, imposing a massive fine of 1,500 talents.

Another section of the walls of Xanthus. In between holocausts at the hands of the Persian and Roman empires the city suffered at the hands of the Greeks, being sacked by Alexander and a bone of contention between his successors. (Courtesy Brian Kohl)

THE REPUBLICAN CONSOLIDATION OF THE EAST

Brutus and Cassius met at Smyrna in late 43 BC. Before seeking to liberate Italy they first resolved to eliminate any potential threats in their rear, specifically Ariobarzanes, king of Cappadocia, the Rhodians and the Lycians.

Cassius was aware Rhodes had maintained her independence against all previous attempts to subjugate her, thwarting the ambitions of Demetrius Poliorketes in 307 BC and Mithridates in 88 BC, so he exercised due diligence in priming his campaign, outfitting and manning his ships carefully and drilling them at Myndus. The Rhodians launched a pre-emptive strike against Cassius with 33 of their best ships, but they were worsted in an engagement off Cos, losing three ships captured with their crews, while two were rammed and sunk.

Cassius then advanced to Loryma, a fortified place belonging to Rhodes on the mainland opposite the island. From this position he sent his infantry across in transports under the command of his lieutenants Fannius and Lentulus while he escorted their convoy in person with 80 ships. A Rhodian naval sortie was beaten back with the loss of two more ships. Having achieved total naval superiority, Cassius prepared to complement the

In seizing Sicily, Sextus Pompey had chosen the ideal redoubt for his outlaw regime; defended on all sides by the Mediterranean, its central location enabled his fleets to intercept the grain transports vital to the subsistence of Rome. Sextus offered shelter to all those disaffected by the Triumvirs' regime, from runaway slaves to the nobility fleeing proscription. (American Numismatic Society)

assault on the landward defences by attacking the sea walls. He had constructed prefabricated siege towers, which were brought on board his ships in sections and then elevated.

This meticulously planned, combined-arms operation was not destined to be consummated as the citizens of Rhodes threw open their gates rather than be subjected to a siege. When some hailed Cassius as lord and king, he answered, that he was neither king nor lord, but the destroyer of both. Imposing a garrison under Lucius Varus, Cassius denuded both public and private funds of Rhodes and then ordered all the other cities and states of Asia to forfeit 10 years' tribute. When news reached him that Cleopatra was about to sail with a large fleet, heavily provisioned, to the Triumvirs, Cassius sent Murcus, with one legion and 60 warships, to the Peloponnese, to lie in wait for her in the vicinity of Taenarum. Afterwards he arrested and executed Ariobarzanes, seizing his large treasure and other military supplies.

After demanding men and supplies from the Lycians Brutus was defied by their popular leader, Naucrates. Brutus scored an initial success when he sent out a party of horse, which surprised a Lycian force while it was at a meal, killing 600 of them. He then defeated the combined army of the Lycians in a pitched battle and when it fled in a body into its camp captured it without a blow. He subsequently set his prisoners free without ransom, hoping to win over the whole nation by evidence of his goodwill. Most cities surrendered but Xanthus continued to defy him; when Brutus established siege lines some of the inhabitants sought to make their escape by diving into the river that flowed by the city, but were taken by nets which had little bells at the top to sound the alarm when anyone was caught in them. Xanthus only fell after savage fighting, which left the city in flames and barely 150 men left alive.

Brutus next advanced on Patara; when his offer of clemency was spurned he set up an auction block at a safe distance under the walls and auctioned off the survivors of Xanthus. Patara finally submitted; at the same time Myra surrendered to Lentulus after he broke the chain that enclosed its harbour, Andriace. The confederation of Lycia now sent ambassadors to Brutus promising to form a military league with him and to contribute what money they could. Brutus ordered the Lycian fleet together with his own ships to set sail for Abydus, where he would rendezvous with his land forces and await Cassius, who was coming from Ionia. The two leaders of the Republican cause met at Sardis in mid-July; having set out for Thrace they arrived at the Hellespont two months later.

OPPOSING PLANS

The strategic situation in 42 BC was almost a carbon copy of that which had confronted Caesar just seven years earlier. At a similar juncture in the Civil War the faction deemed illegitimate by the Senate had seized control of the Republic's western territories while the constitutionalist faction had conceded Rome and recoiled to the Balkans, drawing on the reserves of the East to augment their strength to the point where they could hope to contest for the Republic on equal terms. Deeming it necessary to keep their rivals as far from Rome as possible, the usurpers had braved the enemy's naval superiority to cross the Adriatic and seek a decisive confrontation.

The Republicans hoped to stop history repeating itself through a more effective application of their seapower. Murcus was lying in wait for Cleopatra off the Peloponnesus when he learned that her fleet had been damaged by a storm on the Libyan coast and had limped back to Alexandria, a report confirmed when he saw the wreckage borne by the waves as far as Laconia. Rather than remain idle, on his own recognizance he sailed for Brundisium, anchoring at the island lying opposite the harbour. From this station he prevented the remainder of the Triumvirs' army and supplies from passing over to Macedonia.

Whenever a strong seaward breeze filled the sails of his transports, Antony would embark detachments of his army in a bid to run the blockade piecemeal, supplementing the few warships he had with towers that he mounted on floats in a bid to provide cover. As he fared badly in these encounters, Antony summoned help from Octavian, who was at that time struggling to take possession of his erstwhile province, Sicily.

The Via Egnatia, the great Roman highway running from the Adriatic to Thrace, was the key to control of the Balkans and a bone of contention in the sparring between the Republicans and Triumvirs. (Erich Lessing/Art Resource, NY)

By the year of Philippi, traditional Republican scruples against overt self-propagandization had receded to the point where even Brutus was prepared to defy the ancient taboo against depicting one's own portrait on coins. (Wayne Sayles)

The daggers wielded by Brutus and Cassius here flank a *pileus*, the cap used in the ceremonial emancipation of slaves, thus symbolizing their deliverance of Rome herself from bondage on the ides of March. (Wayne Sayles)

This coin was issued by Brutus to commemorate the double subjugation of Xanthus and Patara, both of which are personified in despair beneath a trophy constructed from the arms and armour of their vanquished defenders.

The sole remaining threat to the Triumvirs' domination of the western Mediterranean was Sextus Pompey. After being falsely condemned under the *lex Pedia*, he had decamped from Massilia with the considerable naval forces under his command and in December 43 BC seized control of Sicily. From this redoubt he offered shelter to those opposed to the new regime, especially those proscribed by the Triumvirs. The support he received from Quintus Cornificius, governor of Africa Vetus, gave the Triumvirs the pretext to endorse the intervention of Titus Sextius, governor of Africa Nova. Cornificius at first held his own but was ultimately overwhelmed, falling in battle.

Octavian was obligated to personally supervise the neutralization of Sextus, who had undertaken a policy of raid and economic blockade of the Italian coastline. He advanced to Rhegium (Reggio Calabria) to link up with his legate Salvidienus Rufus, who had succeeded in forcing Sextus to evacuate his posts in southern Italy. However, in a naval encounter off the Scyllaean promontory in early September, Salvidienus, despite having the larger fleet, had been stymied by the superior nautical skill of the captains serving with Sextus. Unable to affect an amphibious landing in Sicily because he could not command the straits, Octavian finally responded to the urgent appeals of Antony to unite their forces and proceed against Brutus and Cassius. He sailed 'with Sicily on his left,' according to Appian, in other words being forced by Sextus's naval superiority to circumnavigate the island in order to rendezvous with Antony at Brundisium.

On Octavian's approach, Murcus withdrew a short distance from Brundisium in order to avoid being trapped between the Triumvirs. Although he was still on station, Antony and Octavian were able to use a favourable wind to get half their army across the Adriatic. Even more remarkably, although Murcus was waiting to pounce on the empty transports as they made the return voyage, these ships, by luck or daring, were able to collect the rest of the army and then, with full sails, make a second successful shore-to-shore run.

The frustrated Murcus held his position in order to intercept any further convoys bearing the Triumvirs' munitions, supplies and reinforcements. Brutus and Cassius sent Domitius Ahenobarbus with 50 additional ships, one legion and a body of archers to enlarge the Republican naval armada, which had swollen to 130 major warships and even more small ones. This force roamed the Adriatic harassing the enemy at will. It could have achieved more had there been effective cooperation with Sextus, but he was content to fight the Triumvirate on his own terms and never subordinated his interests to those of the Republican cause.

Meanwhile, Gaius Norbanus and Decidius Saxa, whom Octavian and Antony had sent in advance to Macedonia with eight legions, trekked east along the Via Egnatia into Thrace. Norbanus halted at the Sapaei Pass while Saxa advanced more than 100km farther east to secure the Corpili Pass.

Brutus and Cassius crossed the Dardanelles from Abydus to Sestus. Advancing through the Gallipoli Peninsula, at the Gulf of Melas (Saros) the Republican commanders reviewed their army and made a distribution of 1,500 drachmas to each legionary, five times that sum to each centurion. After marching another two days the army came to Aenus and then Doriscus. Further progress was blocked by Saxa's occupation of the Corpili Pass.

Rather than force passage Cassius and Brutus sent Tillius Cimber with the fleet, one legion of troops and some archers to bypass the position by sea, measuring and mapping places suitable for camps and approaching the shore with his ships now and then in order to convince Saxa he had been outflanked. The gambit succeeded; Norbanus urged Saxa to withdraw before he was cut off. As soon as the Corpili Pass was abandoned Brutus and Cassius marched through it.

Norbanus and Saxa strongly fortified the Sapaei Pass, not venturing to offer battle but merely sending out horsemen as skirmishers while dispatching urgent summons to Antony and Octavian. This time the Republicans could find no alternative passage. Given the lateness of the season, they faced the unattractive choice of either risking an assault on an entrenched position or turning in their tracks and withdrawing into Asia.

An unlikely third option then presented itself. The struggle for the future of Rome was taking place on the territory of a Thracian people whose territories extended from the mountain ridge that skirts the Propontis and the southern plains that lie between Mt Rhodope and the sea, including the community of Philippi. They were co-ruled by two clan leaders, the brothers Rhascupolis, who had declared for Cassius, and Rhascus, who had taken up arms for Antony, each bringing with him 3,000 horse.

Rhascupolis advised his allies there was a circuitous route of three days' march north through the hill country that would bring them in the rear of the Sapaei Pass. The route had been considered impassable to men up to that time on account of the rugged terrain, scarcity of water and dense forests. If, however, they could carry their water and carve a trail on the march, by the fourth day they would come to the River Harpessus, which falls into the Nestus, and in one day more they would be at Philippi, flanking the enemy in order to cut him off completely and leave him no chance to retreat.

The Republicans adopted this plan, largely on the grounds there was no other alternative. They sent a detachment in advance guided by Rhascupolis and under the command of Lucius Bibulus. On the fourth day, fatigued and dehydrated, their water nearly exhausted, panic broke out in this advance column; suspecting a ruse, when they saw Rhascupolis riding by and exhorting them to have courage, they reviled him and threw stones at him. In this supreme crisis, Bibulus was able to rally his men and towards evening the river was seen by those in front, who raised a cry of joy that was taken up along the trail until it reached the rear. Brutus and Cassius hurried forwards at once, leading their forces along the freshly cleared trail and advancing to Philippi.

The Republican gambit to trap the Triumvirs' legates at the Sapei only failed because Rhascus, his suspicions aroused by the shouting, made a reconnaissance, located the advance column, and was able to warn Norbanus and Saxa, who abandoned the pass that night and retreated towards Amphipolis. Each of the Thracian brothers received high commendation in their respective army, the one because he had led an army by a secret path, the other because he had discovered the secret.

Brutus is hailed as *imperator* in this coin commemorating his victories over the Thracian tribes – note the trophy display of Thracian arms and armour. (Andreas Pangerl, www.romancoins.info)

Cassius, the alleged autocrat, was in fact more discreet than Brutus, the supposed idealist, and his portrait does not appear on any coins issued in his name, which instead feature the female personification of liberty. (Andreas Pangerl, www.romancoins.info)

THE BATTLES OF PHILIPPI

Having occupied Philippi, Brutus and Cassius based their fleet at Neapolis and established a supply depot on the island of Thasos.

Philippi was founded by and named after Philip II, King of Macedon, on the site of the Thasian colony of Crenides at the foot of Mt Orbelos (the modern Mt Lekani). The city dominated the gap between the hills to the north and a marsh that in antiquity covered the entire plain separating it from the Pangaion Hills to the south. Philip's purpose was twofold; to take control of the neighbouring gold mines and to establish a garrison at a strategic passage between his territory and that of the Thracians. The site controlled the Via Egnatia as it transited from the rugged country to the east to the fertile plain extending to the west. The plain sloped downwards in that direction, making movement easy to those descending from Philippi, but difficult to those going uphill from Amphipolis.

Cassius constructed his camp to take advantage of the slope of Madjiar-tépé, a broad round hillock roughly 500m in diameter, flattened at the top, the summit being 32m above the level of the plain and ideal as both a citadel and observation post. Cassius also stationed a detachment 200m to the south

The harbour at Kavala, ancient Neapolis, the seaport supplying the Republican armies at Philippi. (Author's collection)

LEFT
The approach to Philippi from the north. (Author's collection)

BELOW LEFT
The ruins of Philippi. In 30 BC the city was renamed *Colonia Iulia Philippensis*, and then *Colonia Augusta Iulia Philippensis* after Octavian received the title Augustus from the Senate in January 27 BC. (Author's collection)

of his camp on Kutchuk-tépé, a smaller elevation approximately 400m in length and 200m at most in width, rising no more than 23m in height above the threshold of the marsh.

In his investigation of the terrain Heuzey discovered a very well preserved line of raised ground extending from the base of Madjiar-tépé and running north. The thickness ranged from two metres at the summit to four or five metres at the base. This was the foundation of the Republican palisade connecting Cassius's camp with that of Brutus to the north at the foot of the mountain. Interspersed with gates and towers this fortification was further enhanced by the natural moat of the River Gangites, flowing north to south into the swamp. The Republicans had effectively cut the Via Egnatia.

Between the escarpments and the last slopes down which the Gangites falls there is a 1km stretch of terrain which gradually falls and spreads out into broad terraces barely distinguished by light undulations in the ground. This was the site of Brutus's camp. Militarily, the position offered notable

RIGHT
The ruins of the Basilica of the Apostle Paul, Philippi. The city flourished during the Christian era before being almost totally destroyed by an earthquake around 619 AD. Its residual strategic importance made it a bone of contention between Byzantines, Bulgars and Serbs. (Author's collection)

BELOW RIGHT
Looking west from the acropolis across the ruins of old Philippi and beyond to the site of the clash between the legions of Brutus and Cassius during the first battle. (Author's collection)

advantages. It allowed a panoramic view across the plain, closed the road which led to the least difficult of the passages through the mountains and the shortest way to turn the acropolis of Philippi, and meant Brutus's camp was shielded, like that of Cassius, by the natural barrier of the Gangites.

The drawback to these dispositions was that while the two Republican camps were ideally sited to take advantage of the dominant terrain features in their individual sections of the front they were separated by a gap of 2,700m and incapable of rapid mutual support. The size of this gap would have significant implications for the outcome of the campaign. Such an experienced general as Antony would have immediately recognized the salience of Cassius's camp to the Republican position. It was the key to the entire battlefield, and its isolation encouraged Antony in the belief it could be turned and seized before Brutus could intervene.

Immediately upon landing in Macedonia Antony left Octavian ill at Dyrrachium and marched to secure Amphipolis, unaware it had already been fortified by Norbanus and Saxa. Leaving his supplies there with one legion, under the command of Pinarius, Antony advanced to Philippi and made camp in the plain only 1,500m from the Republican lines.

Antony's audacity, although he was driven to it by necessity, confounded the enemy when they saw him pitch his camp so near them and in such a contemptuous manner as soon as he arrived. He raised numerous towers and fortified himself on all sides with ditches, wall and palisade. The Republicans also worked to cover any blind spots left in their defences. Most significantly, Cassius extended his lines to cover the gap between his camp and the marsh, a space which had been overlooked on account of its narrowness, so that there was now nothing unfortified except the cliffs on Brutus's right flank and the marsh on Cassius's left.

THE ORDERS OF BATTLE

In the words of Plutarch, never had two such large Roman armies come together to engage each other. The Triumvirs' army at Philippi (not counting the legion stationed at Amphipolis) totalled 19 legions, roughly 110,000 men. The sources report specifically the name of only one legion, the IV, but others likely present included the veteran VI, VII, VIII, X Equestris and perhaps the XII, and the newer III, XXVI, XXVIII, XXIX, and XXX, all of which participated in the land settlements after the battle. The Triumvirs' cavalry force consisted of 13,000 horsemen contributed by allied and subject peoples, primarily Spaniards, Gauls and Germans.

The Republican army had 17 legions, eight with Brutus and nine with Cassius (not counting two more being stationed with the fleet, one with Ahenobarbus, one with Murcus), roughly 90,000 men. The backbone of the army comprised the old Caesarean legions stationed in the east after Pharsalus – definitely the XXVII, XXXVI and XXXVII, and probably the XXXI and XXXIII.

To find suitable officers Brutus recruited among the young Romans studying in Athens, including the poet Horace. Only two of the legions were at full strength, the army being reinforced by levies from the Eastern allied kingdoms, such as a troop of Galatian infantry under their tetrarchs that could not have consisted of fewer than 5,000 men. The Republican cavalry was 17,000 strong; Brutus had 4,000 Gallic and Lusitanian horse, and 2,000 Thracian, Illyrian, Parthian and Thessalian; Cassius had 2,000 Spanish and Gallic and 5,000 Galatian horse, and 4,000 Arab, Mede and Parthian mounted archers.

The Republican army was therefore both smaller and more heterogeneous than that of the Triumvirs, a dangerous combination. This polyglot nature is illustrated by a breakdown of the detachments serving under Brutus. Since departing Italy little more than a year earlier he had accrued the following: the three depleted legions under Vatinius in Illyria; the legion under Antony's legate Piso, the last remaining of the six originally stationed in Macedonia; those cohorts under Antony's brother Gaius that held out at Apollonia after Piso surrendered; stragglers from the legion Dolabella had taken from Macedonia to Asia; Pompeian survivors from Pharsalus; volunteers from Italy; Roman residents in Macedonia, Illyria and Greece; and two *legiones vernaculae* recruited from native Macedonians.

Furthermore, the loyalty of the backbone of their army, the veteran soldiers under their command who were supposed to fight against Caesar's heir and right hand man, was a delicate issue for Brutus and Cassius. They laboured to reinforce the allegiance of their men, both with monetary bonuses and with passionate speeches emphasizing civic pride and Republican virtues: 'Let it give no one any concern that he has been one of Caesar's soldiers,' Cassius insisted, 'We were not his soldiers then, but our country's.'

THE OPENING MOVES

Whatever advantages the Triumvirs retained at the tactical level, the strategic superiority of the Republican position was immediately apparent. The Republicans were on elevated ground, the Triumvirs on the plain; the Republicans procured fuel from the mountains, the Triumvirs from the marsh; the Republicans obtained water from the river, the Triumvirs from freshly dug wells; the Republicans had a secure depot on Thasos, while the Triumvirs were 65km from the nearest urban centre under their control, Amphipolis; with their naval superiority and ruthlessly amassed treasure trove the Republicans could draw on supplies of grain and fodder from virtually anywhere in the Mediterranean, while the Triumvirs were entirely dependent on the local surpluses of Macedonia and Thessaly, which would not suffice for long.

For a time Antony's prestige was a source of inspiration to his soldiers, but after laying an ambush for some of the enemy when they were gathering grain and failing in the attempt, even he lost heart. When Octavian heard Antony had made contact with the Republicans he knew he could not afford to be absent from any ensuing clash of arms, for if Brutus and Cassius had the victory he could not defy them alone, whereas if Antony triumphed single-handedly his ascendancy would be so complete none would dare challenge his claim to the legacy of Caesar. Although still sick, Octavian hastened to link up with his partner, arriving at Philippi 10 days after Antony.

Every day the Triumvirs would go through the motions of assembling their army and offering battle; Brutus and Cassius would also draw out their forces on their higher ground, in order not to lose face, or depress the fighting

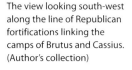

The view looking south-west along the line of Republican fortifications linking the camps of Brutus and Cassius. (Author's collection)

The approach to Philippi

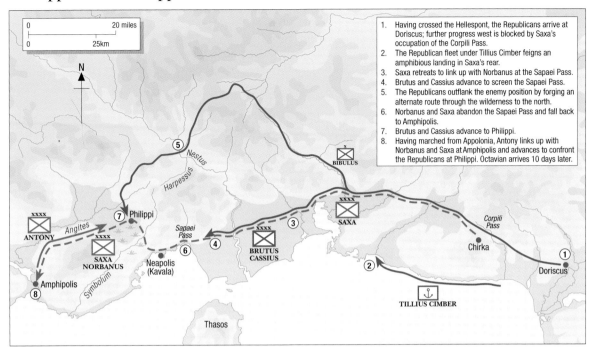

1. Having crossed the Hellespont, the Republicans arrive at Doriscus; further progress west is blocked by Saxa's occupation of the Corpili Pass.
2. The Republican fleet under Tillius Cimber feigns an amphibious landing in Saxa's rear.
3. Saxa retreats to link up with Norbanus at the Sapaei Pass.
4. Brutus and Cassius advance to screen the Sapaei Pass.
5. The Republicans outflank the enemy position by forging an alternate route through the wilderness to the north.
6. Norbanus and Saxa abandon the Sapaei Pass and fall back to Amphipolis.
7. Brutus and Cassius advance to Philippi.
8. Having marched from Appolonia, Antony links up with Norbanus and Saxa at Amphipolis and advances to confront the Republicans at Philippi. Octavian arrives 10 days later.

spirit of their men, but they never advanced into the plain. They were prepared to fight a war of attrition. They would wait out the autumn and when winter came, and the Triumvirs were forced by hunger to retreat, the Republicans would harass their enervated enemy every step of the way, ideally cutting them to pieces on the march, if necessary driving them into Amphipolis and starving them into submission there.

Fully appreciating that an enemy so aware of the natural superiority of its defensive position would never willingly offer battle, in late September Antony resolved to force the issue and leave the Republicans no alternative. His plan was to construct a passage through the marsh – secretly, if possible – in order to get in the enemy's rear without their knowledge and cut off their supply route to Thasos. He continued to array his forces for battle every morning with all their standards displayed, so that it might seem that his entire army was drawn up, but in reality he was working night and day to force a narrow passage through the marsh. His engineers cut down reeds to serve as the foundation for a causeway, flanking it with stone, so that the earth should not fall away, and bridging the deeper parts with piles, all in the profoundest silence. The reeds left standing prevented the enemy from detecting his progress. After working 10 days in this manner he sent a column of troops under cover of darkness to occupy all the fortified positions already incorporated within his lines and build several additional redoubts.

THE FIRST BATTLE OF PHILIPPI

Finally alerted to the threat, Cassius immediately put in place a counter-strategy intended to cut Antony off from his advance working parties. He ordered construction of a transverse wall stretching from his camp into the marsh with the intention of cutting through the passage made by Antony at

The site of the Triumvirs' camp, viewed from the north-east. The strategic vulnerability of the site – its exposure to Republican observers on the heights – is immediately apparent. (Author's collection)

a right angle, so that those inside could not escape to him, nor he render assistance to them. The isolated strongpoints could then be mopped up.

When Antony discerned Cassius's intent around noon on 3 October, he turned the right wing of his army and led it against the transverse wall of Cassius in the space between his camp and the marsh. Antony ordered tools and ladders brought up with the assault force, intending to take the transverse wall by storm and then force his way into Cassius's camp.

Charging obliquely and uphill under a shower of missiles Antony forced his way until he struck the left flank of Cassius, which had not moved from its assigned position and was amazed at this unexpected audacity. He broke this advance guard and swarmed against the transverse wall, demolished the palisade, filled up the ditch, undermined the works, and killed the men at the gates, disregarding the missiles hurled from the wall, until he had forced an entrance and others had made breaches in the fortification, and still others had climbed up on the debris. All this was done so swiftly that those who had just now captured the fortification met Cassius's men, who had been at work in the marsh, coming to the assistance of their comrades. With a powerful charge Antony's men put them to flight, drove them back into the marsh, and then at once wheeled against the camp of Cassius itself. These were only the men who had scaled the fortification with Antony, the bulk of his army being engaged with Cassius's remaining legions on the far side of the wall.

As the camp was in a strong position it was guarded by only a few men, and Antony easily overcame them. Cassius's soldiers on the plain were already being beaten, and when they saw that their camp was taken they scattered in disorderly flight.

Antony's triumph was offset by the disaster that befell his junior colleague. Octavian had drawn out his army in support of Antony, but was too ill to command his men in person and his soldiers, expecting the enemy not to seek a set battle but instead only to make some excursions with missile weapons and light arms to disturb the men at work in the trenches, were caught off guard when they heard the sound of full-scale battle echoing to the south.

Brutus was in the process of distributing to his officers their orders to advance when some of his legions, perhaps sensing the hesitation and lack of

direction in the ranks opposite, impulsively charged, drawing the entire army after them. This disorder caused unevenness in the line, with the legions becoming separated from one another. This worked to Brutus's advantage. First the legion under the command of Messala Corvinus on the far right of his line, and then the one adjoining it, passed beyond Octavian's left wing and crashed directly into the Triumvirs' camp, indiscriminately slaughtering the occupants, including all 2,000 of the Spartans who had just arrived in response to the appeals of Octavian.

The bulk of Brutus's troops meanwhile engaged Octavian's army and easily routed it, according to Plutarch wiping out three legions; Appian relates Brutus commending his men after the battle for having 'utterly destroyed their far-famed IV legion on which their wing placed its reliance.' Upon pursuing those that fled into the camp, some of his men showed Brutus their bloody swords and declared they had killed Octavian, describing his person and his age. Others among those Republicans who stormed the camp had pierced his litter, which was left empty, in many places. The rumour spread like lightning that Octavian was slain, but the adopted son of Caesar had in fact taken refuge in the marsh. Octavian, as he himself admitted in his now lost memoirs, had been conveyed away only just in time, having been urged not to remain in camp by Marcus Artorius, his physician, who had been frightened by a warning that had appeared to him in a dream.

The battle ended in mass and universal confusion, with the losers in flight and the victors engaged in plundering the camps they had seized. Because of the extent of the plain and the immense quantities of dust kicked up, both sides were ignorant of the outcome of the battle. The victorious legionaries from both sides began to filter back towards their respective camps; according to Appian, they 'resembled porters rather than soldiers' under the weight of the loot they had amassed.

Brutus received his first hint that something was amiss in the camp of his partner when he realized he could not see Cassius's tent standing above the rest, for it had been immediately pulled down and pillaged by the enemy. Those with keener eyes confirmed there was a great deal of activity in Cassius's camp, and that, by their number and the fashion of their armour,

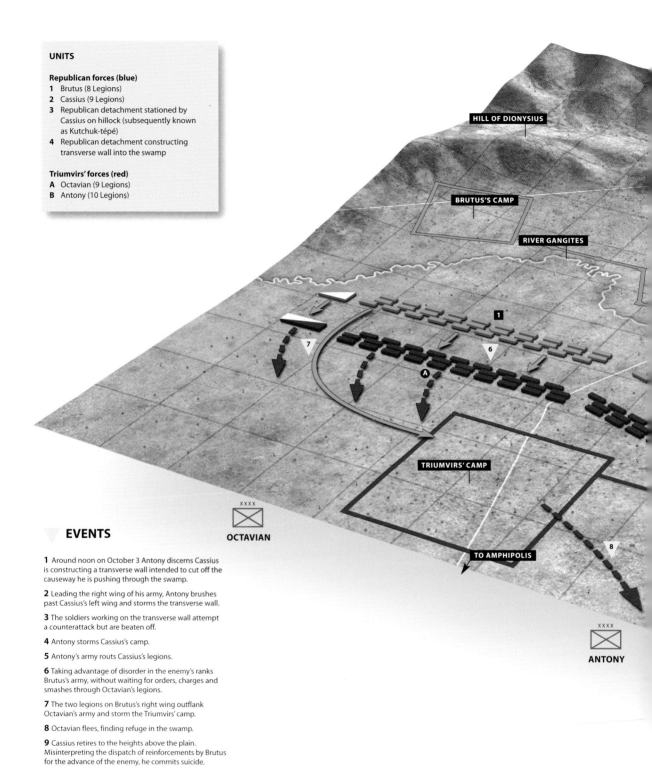

UNITS

Republican forces (blue)
1 Brutus (8 Legions)
2 Cassius (9 Legions)
3 Republican detachment stationed by Cassius on hillock (subsequently known as Kutchuk-tépé)
4 Republican detachment constructing transverse wall into the swamp

Triumvirs' forces (red)
A Octavian (9 Legions)
B Antony (10 Legions)

HILL OF DIONYSIUS

BRUTUS'S CAMP

RIVER GANGITES

TRIUMVIRS' CAMP

TO AMPHIPOLIS

XXXX
OCTAVIAN

XXXX
ANTONY

EVENTS

1 Around noon on October 3 Antony discerns Cassius is constructing a transverse wall intended to cut off the causeway he is pushing through the swamp.

2 Leading the right wing of his army, Antony brushes past Cassius's left wing and storms the transverse wall.

3 The soldiers working on the transverse wall attempt a counterattack but are beaten off.

4 Antony storms Cassius's camp.

5 Antony's army routs Cassius's legions.

6 Taking advantage of disorder in the enemy's ranks Brutus's army, without waiting for orders, charges and smashes through Octavian's legions.

7 The two legions on Brutus's right wing outflank Octavian's army and storm the Triumvirs' camp.

8 Octavian flees, finding refuge in the swamp.

9 Cassius retires to the heights above the plain. Misinterpreting the dispatch of reinforcements by Brutus for the advance of the enemy, he commits suicide.

THE FIRST BATTLE OF PHILIPPI, 3 OCTOBER 42 BC

At the first battle of Philippi, Brutus defeated Octavian, while Cassius's forces were overcome by those of Antony. Cassius committed suicide as a result. At the same time as the battle was raging, the Triumvirs' reinforcements under Calvinus were annihilated while crossing the Adriatic by a Republican fleet under Murcus and Ahenobarbus.

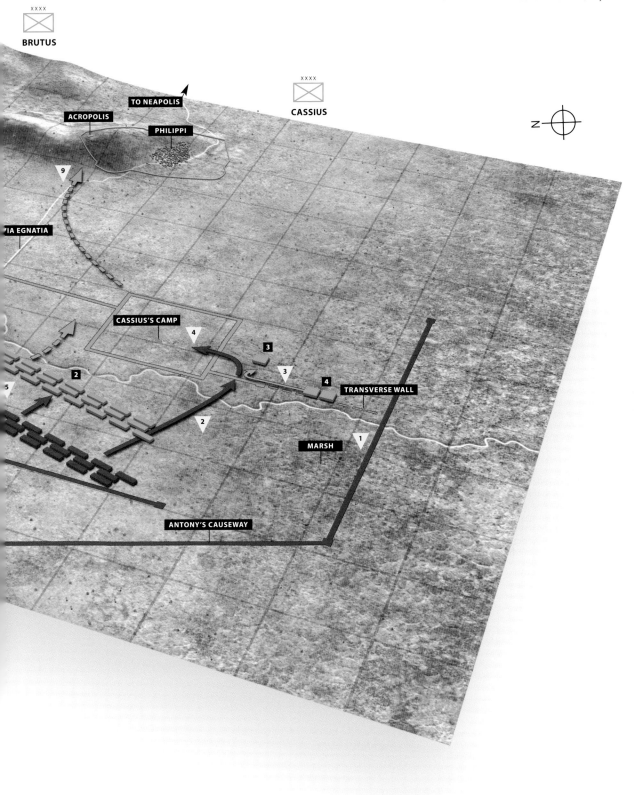

Note: Gridlines are shown at intervals of 500m/547yds

BRUTUS

CASSIUS

TO NEAPOLIS

ACROPOLIS

PHILIPPI

VIA EGNATIA

9

CASSIUS'S CAMP

4

3

3

4

TRANSVERSE WALL

2

5

2

1

MARSH

ANTONY'S CAUSEWAY

N

59

the soldiers milling about could not be the Republicans left on guard. Alerted to the misfortune of the Republican left flank Brutus stationed a guard in the Triumvirs' camp, recalled the pursuit of Octavian's scattered legions, marshalled his forces and led them to the relief of Cassius, sending a detachment of cavalry on ahead.

When Cassius saw his line was beginning to give way he had snatched a standard out of the hand of its bearer and stuck it at his feet in a bid to serve as a rallying point. This gambit failed; he could hardly keep even his own personal guard together, so at last he was forced to retreat with a few retainers to the acropolis of Philippi overlooking the plain. From these heights the small cluster of Republicans saw the great body of horse Brutus had sent moving towards them. Cassius believed these were hostile, and in pursuit of him; however, to confirm this he sent one of his confederates, Titinius.

As soon as Brutus's horse saw him coming, those acquainted with Titinius began shouting with joy; alighting from their horses, they shook hands and embraced him, while the rest rode round about him singing. Cassius, however, interpreted the hubbub to mean Titinius had been captured by the enemy. Lamenting that his greed for life had only resulted in being forced to endure 'the sight of my friend taken by the enemy before my face', he withdrew, taking only Pindarus, one of his freedmen. Moments later his head was found lying severed from the body. Thus Cassius's life ended on his birthday. Titinius, crowned with the garlands of victory, had hastened to bring the glad tidings to Cassius. As soon as he realized he was too late he drew his sword, and, 'having very much accused and upbraided' his own failure to report the truth in time, he too killed himself.

According to conjecture, the ancient sources tell us, Cassius lost approximately 9,000 men, not all of them combat troops, but including the slaves and other unfortunates trapped within his camp when Antony forced the gates. Octavian is supposed to have lost double that number. Plutarch comments that the distinction between the outmanned left flanks of each army was that while Octavian's soldiers were killed where they stood most of Cassius's soldiers had fled rather than be overwhelmed.

The honours appeared even in the wake of the first battle, and the strategic situation appeared unchanged, as both sides, concerned at the possibility of overstretching their lines, abandoned the camps they had seized and fell back on their original positions. In fact, with Cassius dead, the balance had shifted dramatically in favour of the Triumvirs.

THE SECOND BATTLE OF PHILIPPI

Brutus, who feared the impact on morale that a public burial of his colleague would entail, immediately sent the body of Cassius secretly to be interred on Thasos. He then spent the whole night, without food and without care for his own person, restoring order in Cassius's army. Formally assuming command of the remnant of Cassius's legions the next day, he consoled them in a speech, won their devotion by a gift of 2,000 drachmas per man to make up for what they had lost in the pillage of their tents, and then transferred his flag to their camp in recognition of its greater strategic significance.

Antony likewise assumed sole authority over the Triumvirs' legions; Pliny the Elder refers to Octavian, though still suffering from sickness, having to remain concealed in the marsh for three days before being able slink back into camp. Antony had been made aware of the demise of the senior Republican commander on the evening of the battle when a former servant of Cassius named Demetrius came to him bringing the garment he had taken from the body of his dead master, and his sword. Encouraged, Antony offered battle the following day, urging his men not to lose heart at their camp being despoiled, 'for wealth consists not in the property we hold, but in conquering with might, which will restore to us as victors not only what we lost yesterday, which is still safe in the enemy's possession, but the enemy's wealth in addition. And if we are in haste to take these things let us hasten to bring on a battle.'

Brutus led his men out but refused to descend to the plain and risk a second trial of strength. He was determined to adhere to the original strategy of attrition, reminding his officers that while their enemy might be eager to

ANTONY VICTORIOUS AT THE FIRST BATTLE OF PHILIPPI (pp. 62–63)

The First Battle of Philippi was initiated when Cassius, alerted to the threat of his lines being outflanked by Antony, ordered construction of a transverse wall stretching from his camp into the marsh. When Antony detected this activity around noon on October 3 he turned the right wing of his army and led it in a charge. Antony (1) is depicted here resplendent in his scarlet *paludamentum*, the scarlet cloak of a general. He is accompanied by a trumpeter (cornicen, 2) and standard-bearer (signifer, 3), vital to retaining command and control in the fluid environment of close combat. Antony had ordered his strike force to retain their entrenching tools (4) in addition to having ladders (5) brought up for the assault. Upon contact with the transverse wall his men filled up the ditch (6) and demolished the palisade (7), swarming over or through the fortifications

so swiftly they routed Cassius's work parties who were rushing to the assistance of their comrades, driving them back into the marsh (8), and then immediately wheeling against Cassius's camp. In leading a handful of men in oblique charge across the face of massed enemy forces against an entrenched position Antony had taken a massive gamble, but on this occasion fortune truly favoured the brave. Cassius's camp was overrun and his field army, engaged with the bulk of Antony's legions, subsequently folded. Antony's triumph not only mitigated the disaster meted out to his junior colleague at the other end of the Triumviral line, it precipitated the suicide of Cassius, ensuring the Triumvirs would subsequently retain the strategic initiative.

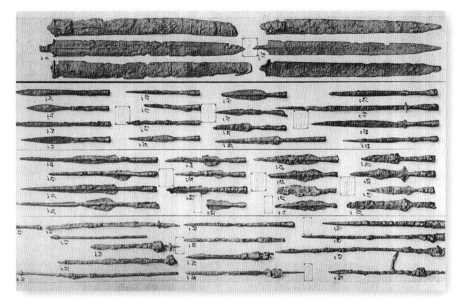

In the aftermath of the battles at Philippi the ground would have been strewn with discarded weapons of the same type as these models recovered during excavation at Alesia. The poet Virgil aptly summed up the terms under which the last stand of the Republic would take place: 'And so Philippi again saw Roman armies in battle, fighting among themselves with equal weapons'.

fight, 'bear in mind that they are so pressed by hunger that they prefer death by battle. We will make it part of our plan that hunger shall engage them before we do; so that when it is necessary to fight we shall find them weakened and exhausted. Let us not be carried away by our ardour before the proper time.'

It was a sound strategy. Given their already straitened circumstances prior to the battle, the condition of the Triumvirs' camp, after being ransacked by Brutus, could have offered little comfort to its original owners upon repossession. The situation further deteriorated when a heavy autumn rain fell after the battle. The camp was in low ground, and so its tents all filled with mire and water, which immediately froze. It was a harbinger of what to expect during the rapidly approaching winter. In addition to running short of food, both Antony and Octavian were out of money and consequently could only compensate their soldiers for the possessions they had lost in the pillage of their camp with extravagant promises of rewards as a corollary of victory. Morale suffered another body blow when word arrived of a disaster that had befallen the Triumvirs' cause on the same day as the first battle at Philippi. A convoy of reinforcements, including two legions, cavalry and auxiliaries, that embarked from Brundisium under Domitius Calvinus had been intercepted and annihilated in the Adriatic by the Republican admirals Ahenobarbus and Murcus. The only mitigating concession the Triumvirs could extract from this catastrophe was preventing news of it from reaching Brutus. It wasn't until the evening prior to the second battle that a deserter named Clodius brought word that the Triumvirs were aware of the loss of their fleet, and for that reason were desperately seeking a decisive confrontation. But his story met with no credit, nor was he so much as seen by Brutus, being written off as either an agent deliberately spreading misinformation or a defector inventing lies to win favour.

Brutus never intended for his strategy of attrition to mean remaining in an entirely passive defensive posture; he deployed various stratagems to continue harassing the Triumvirs, from assaulting their positions at night to on one occasion diverting the course of the river and washing away a considerable part of their camp.

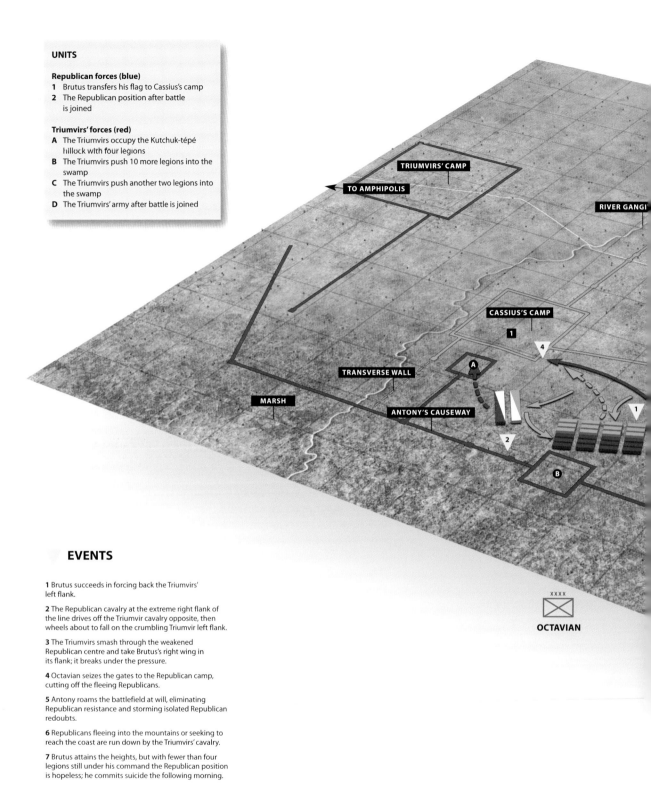

UNITS

Republican forces (blue)
1   Brutus transfers his flag to Cassius's camp
2   The Republican position after battle
    is joined

Triumvirs' forces (red)
A   The Triumvirs occupy the Kutchuk-tépé
    hillock with four legions
B   The Triumvirs push 10 more legions into the
    swamp
C   The Triumvirs push another two legions into
    the swamp
D   The Triumvirs' army after battle is joined

TRIUMVIRS' CAMP

TO AMPHIPOLIS

RIVER GANGI

CASSIUS'S CAMP

TRANSVERSE WALL

MARSH

ANTONY'S CAUSEWAY

XXXX

OCTAVIAN

EVENTS

1 Brutus succeeds in forcing back the Triumvirs'
left flank.

2 The Republican cavalry at the extreme right flank of
the line drives off the Triumvir cavalry opposite, then
wheels about to fall on the crumbling Triumvir left flank.

3 The Triumvirs smash through the weakened
Republican centre and take Brutus's right wing in
its flank; it breaks under the pressure.

4 Octavian seizes the gates to the Republican camp,
cutting off the fleeing Republicans.

5 Antony roams the battlefield at will, eliminating
Republican resistance and storming isolated Republican
redoubts.

6 Republicans fleeing into the mountains or seeking to
reach the coast are run down by the Triumvirs' cavalry.

7 Brutus attains the heights, but with fewer than four
legions still under his command the Republican position
is hopeless; he commits suicide the following morning.

THE SECOND BATTLE OF PHILIPPI, 23 OCTOBER 42 BC

At the second battle of Philippi, Antony and Octavian's forces combined to break through the Republican lines.
The Triumvirs swung to their left to take Brutus in his flank and rear. Brutus fled to the heights to the north of
Philippi, where recognizing his situation to be without hope, he committed suicide the following day.

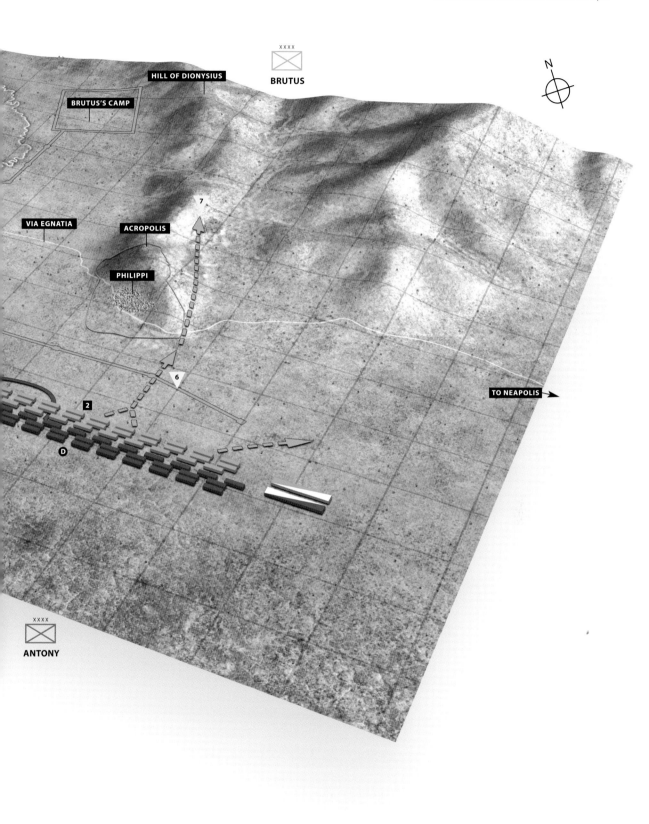

N

XXXX
BRUTUS

HILL OF DIONYSIUS

BRUTUS'S CAMP

7

VIA EGNATIA

ACROPOLIS

PHILIPPI

6

TO NEAPOLIS

2

D

XXXX
ANTONY

The strategic situation facing Antony and Octavian was becoming desperate. Hunger was already felt, Thessaly could no longer furnish sufficient supplies, nor could they hope for anything to arrive by sea. A legion of troops was dispatched to Achaia to collect all the food available, but the entire army would have to be dispersed in this manner for it to survive the winter and in doing so it would lose all capacity for offensive action. It was now obvious there was no alternative to forcing a decisive confrontation with Brutus. As the daily ritual of offering battle was obviously an exercise in futility, the Triumvirs instead resorted to psychological warfare, advancing to the Republican fortifications, challenging Brutus to fight, reviling and scoffing at him, and doing everything possible to provoke him, or at least his men, into a second fight.

According to the classic accounts it was this campaign of systematic provocation that succeeded in cajoling the Republican army, against the better judgement of Brutus, into giving Antony the stand-up fight he wanted. But it is important to bear in mind the classic accounts are biased by their desire to conform to the demands of a literary construct that required symmetry between the battles of Pharsalus and Philippi. In both instances the Republican defeat was ascribed to the Republican general being swept into a decisive battle he considered unnecessary because he could not control the factional infighting at his camp. This perspective was intended to reflect the decadence of the Republic itself, thereby rationalizing its being usurped by the principate. The analogy was made explicit by Appian, who quotes Brutus, after having submitted to the rash enthusiasm of his subordinates, lamenting: 'I seem likely to carry on war like Pompey the Great, not so much commanding now as commanded.'

In some respects the classic accounts do reflect the strategic reality of the Republican situation after the first battle. Brutus does seem to have failed to fully integrate the legions he inherited from Cassius with his own; Plutarch notes that those of Cassius's soldiers who had survived the first battle

Another depiction of a merchant ship. With a favourable wind these vessels were capable of running a blockade, but if the wind dropped they would be at the mercy of oar-powered warships. (Erich Lessing/Art Resource, NY)

'infected the other and larger part of the army with their want of spirit and their disorder.' The nagging concern that many of the legionaries under his command remained in their hearts closer to the heirs of Caesar than the Republican cause, especially now in the absence of the forceful Cassius, did have a basis in reality as there was a slow drip-feed of defections to the Triumvirs. Increasing pressure was placed on Brutus, both by what Appian stigmatizes as the 'unreasoning multitude' of his rank and file, who 'without reflection' began more and more openly to demand the consummation of his first victory, and his officers who, sensing the mood of the men, lobbied for a second trial of arms. Ultimately, Appian relates that Brutus, 'contrary to his dignity,' yielded to their demands, 'to the ruin of himself and them.'

The problem with the classic accounts is that the parallels with Pharsalus have broken down at this point. There really was no need for Pompey to risk battle with Caesar, but in fact Brutus had been left with no option but to confront Antony.

Antony's attempt to turn the southern flank of the Republican defences had precipitated the first battle, and control over access to and transit through the swamp remained the crucible of the entire theatre of operations. In seeking to exploit it, Antony was able to take advantage of a major tactical blunder on the part of Brutus. Just south of Cassius's camp on Madjiar-tépé was a smaller rise called Kutchuk-tépé. Although it was within bowshot of his camp and could be covered by his archers, Cassius had placed a guard on it to deter the Triumvirs from attempting to seize it. For some unknown reason, after taking sole command of the Republican army Brutus elected to withdraw this garrison. The Triumvirs promptly occupied the hillock by night with four legions, which erected wickerwork and screens as cover against the Republican archers when they were detected at dawn. When this position was secured, they stationed another 10 legions nearly a kilometre into the marsh, then pushed an additional two legions three-

THE TRIUMVIRAL REINFORCEMENTS ARE ANNIHILATED AT SEA (pp. 70–71)

On the same day as the First Battle of Philippi, another great calamity took place in the Adriatic. Attempting to reinforce the Triumvirs, Domitius Calvinus had embarked from Brundisium with two legions (including the Martian), a praetorian cohort of about 2,000 men, four squadrons of horse, and a considerable body of other troops. This bid to run the gauntlet of the Republican blockade failed; Murcus and Ahenobarbus with 130 warships intercepted the convoy en route. A few of the leading transports got away under sail but when the wind suddenly failed the rest were trapped in a dead calm. Brushing aside the handful of escorts (1) the Republican galleys swooped upon the transports. In desperation the transport captains warped their ships together with ropes and reinforced them with spars to prevent the enemy from breaking through their line. In response Murcus subjected them to a barrage of flaming missiles (2). When the transports separated in order to prevent the flames from spreading they again left themselves exposed to being shot to pieces or rammed. Some of the doomed legionaries, especially the Martians, killed themselves rather than be burned

to death; others leaped on board the Republican galleys, selling their lives dearly. Such an eventuality is depicted in this scene.

A Republican quinquireme (3) has ventured too close to its prey, a heavy transport ship (4). Seizing their opportunity, the surviving Triumviral legionaries, many having discarded their armour and even helmets, are leaping from their vessel (5), exploiting the higher free board of the transport relative to the quinquireme. Others, knowing their only chance of coming to grips with the enemy is to ensure the conflict is hand-to-hand, use hooks to bind the two vessels together (6). A vicious struggle has erupted around one of the ballistas (7) located near the quinquireme's bow.

Most of the transports ultimately surrendered, as did 17 of their escorts, which were drafted into the Republican fleet. Calvinus, who was believed to have perished, returned to Brundisium five days later, but there was no disguising the extent of the disaster, or its implications; cut off from the rest of the Roman world, Antony and Octavian would either triumph or lose all at Philippi.

quarters of a kilometre farther east. Brutus counteracted this movement by building fortified posts opposite their camps.

Antony was taking a considerable risk; by advancing all of the Triumvirs' 16 legions through the swamp he had effectively denuded the defences of his camp, which can only have been held by his cavalry and a screening force of auxiliaries. But Brutus was now in danger of his entire position being isolated and rendered untenable. If the Triumvirs were allowed to continue stretching their lines unimpeded, they would ultimately cut off his supply route to Neapolis and pin him against the mountains. If that happened, the tables would be turned; he would either be starved into submission or be forced to retreat by taking his entire army via the hazardous northern trail that had brought him to Philippi.

This, then, is the real background to the second battle. Brutus may have been as reluctant to risk going toe-to-toe with Antony as the classic accounts depict, but if so those Republicans who forced his hand were not acting irrationally but exhibiting a much sounder understanding of the strategic situation than their commander.

Again, the accounts of our three sources are difficult to reconcile. All agree that Brutus remained in a conservative frame of mind when he led out his army and formed it up in line of battle before his walls, ordering them not to advance too far down the slope in order to retain a good position for hurling missiles at the enemy, and in order to effect an orderly retreat if necessary. In a grim reflection of the fratricidal nature of the conflict, since he lacked the manpower to guard the many captives in his camp and could not trust them to refrain from attempting some mischief once the battle ensued, Brutus put the majority of them to death. According to Dio, he felt justified in making this decision because the Triumvirs had executed those Republicans captured after the first battle.

According to Plutarch, Brutus was still reluctant to fight, for even with his army in battle array rumours of disloyalty still persisted, accusations of secret affiliation with the Triumvirs being levelled against some men. In addition, his cavalry was not eager to begin the action and was waiting for the infantry to make the first move. Suddenly, Camulatus, whom Plutarch describes as 'a very good soldier, and one whom for his valour he highly esteemed, riding hard by Brutus himself, went over to the enemy.' Partly out of anger, and partly out of fear this brazen defection would provoke further desertion, Brutus finally authorized a full-scale assault. It was now three o'clock in the afternoon.

According to Dio, the two sides had little need for missile weapons, 'for they did not resort to the usual manoeuvres and tactics of battles,' but immediately advanced to close combat, 'seeking to break each other's ranks.' His depiction of the two armies immediately coming to grips accords well with the incredibly constricted nature of the combat environment. The narrow space left between the two rival east–west-running parallel lines of fortifications, especially considering the size of the forces engaged, surely constitutes the most cramped battlefield conditions in antiquity – the ideal circumstances for compression panic to erupt in whichever army lost its nerve first. Dio's account effectively encapsulates the nature of Roman warfare:

> The bodies of the fallen were carried back and others stepped into their places from the reserves. The generals flew hither and thither overlooking everything, exciting the men by their ardour, exhorting the toilers to toil on, and relieving those who were exhausted so that there was always fresh courage at the front.

Gnaeus Domitius Ahenobarbus was the son of one of Caesar's most obdurate foes, Lucius Domitius Ahenobarbus. After Philippi he continued to defy Octavian, first independently and then in the service of Antony.

Lucius Statius Murcus, depicted here raising the kneeling figure of Asia, had served as a legate to Caesar during the first civil war, being one of the three commissioners appointed by him to treat with the Pompeians at Oricum. The tangle of conflicting loyalties following the ides of March led him into the service of Cassius and ultimately into the camp of Sextus Pompey.

Dio does not discuss the tactical ramifications of the battle in any detail, merely stating Brutus 'was defeated after a long and close struggle, and then, when many had fallen, his cavalry also gave way, though it fought nobly.' Plutarch is more specific. In his account, Brutus had the better of the fight at the western end of his line and pressed hard on the Triumvirs' left wing, which gave way and retreated, being harassed by the Republican cavalry, which sought to exploit the advantage when it saw the enemy in disorder. But the eastern flank of the Republican line, its numbers being inferior, had been extended to avoid being outflanked. This meant the Republican legions had been drawn out too thin in the centre, and were so weak here they could not withstand the Triumvirs' initial charge. Having broken through, the Triumvirs swung to their left to take Brutus in his flank and rear.

Appian speaks of the Triumvirs' legions having 'pushed back the enemy's line as though they were turning round a very heavy machine.' The Republicans were driven back step-by-step, slowly at first, but as their ranks crumbled under the pressure they began to give ground more rapidly. The second and third reserve lines in the rear failed to keep pace with the retreat and all three lines became entangled, individual cohorts being crowded into each other by the unrelenting advance of the enemy. This was the scenario every commander dreaded. As each legionary felt his safe zone of personal freedom being compromised panic would set in, discipline would collapse and unit cohesion would be lost. The legion would degenerate from a corporate, hierarchical entity that was responsive to a chain of command into a mob of individuals making self-interested fight or flight decisions on an entirely ad hoc basis.

The Republican army was now subjected to just this process of fragmentation. Some stood their ground, particularly the young idealists who had aligned themselves with Brutus during his sojourn in Athens. Prominent among them was Marcus Cato. His family and the Republican tradition being synonymous, Plutarch relates: 'He would neither fly nor give the least ground, but, still fighting and declaring who he was and naming his father's name, he fell upon a heap of dead bodies of the enemy. And of the rest, the bravest were slain in defending Brutus.' But most obeyed baser instincts, among them

Looking north from the Triumvirs' front line at the commencement of the second battle. (Author's collection)

Horace, who ruefully recollected many years later that 'I experienced Philippi and a speedy flight, abandoning my poor little shield indecorously.'

Octavian's men, following specific orders, seized the gates of the Republican camp. Though at great risk because they were exposed to missiles from above and in front, they prevented many Republican refugees from securing shelter behind its walls. Leaving Octavian to prevent anyone breaking into, or out of, the Republican headquarters, Antony relentlessly scoured the battlefield, harrying the fugitives, breaking up attempts by knots of Republicans to rally and make a stand, and storming the outlying Republican redoubts.

His priority was the Republican leadership; determined to prevent them from slipping away and raising another army he dispersed his cavalry to run to ground those trying to escape either to the higher ground or to the sea. A picked body of men was led up the mountain by the Thracian Rhascus, who

Every detail in this 16th-century Flemish tapestry, now hanging in the Patrimonio Nacional, Madrid, is anachronistic, but it does capture the dynamism of Antony, the focal point of both battles at Philippi.

had local knowledge of the roads. Their chief quarry was Brutus, but he and a still considerable force were able to find temporary refuge in the heights where the peaks of Panaghir-dagh shelter a depression today occupied by the hamlets of Isabola and Kidjilik at either end of a deep ravine.

Antony passed the night under arms with his outposts aligned against Brutus's original camp, fortifying himself with a breastwork of dead bodies and the spoils of war. Octavian retained command until midnight and then retired on account of his illness, leaving Norbanus to watch Cassius's camp.

Brutus took stock the following morning. He could see the enemy lying in wait for him, and the only forces under his direct command were the fewer than four full legions which had ascended the mountain with him. He conferred with his officers to get their assessment of whether it was still possible to break through the enemy's lines and regain their camp, which was still held by its garrison. The response was entirely negative, the consensus being that those who could still expect mercy were now prepared to seek terms, and that they would not throw away the last remaining hope of accommodation in a futile attempt to revive a lost cause.

Brutus abandoned hope; in Dio's account, 'despairing of safety and disdaining capture, he also took refuge in death.' Suetonius relates Octavian sending Brutus' head to Rome to be cast at the feet of the statue of Caesar; Dio says it was Antony who ordered that his body receive burial but his head be sent to Rome, but, as the ships carrying it encountered a storm during the voyage across from Dyrrachium, it was thrown into the sea. Appian, on the other hand, relates that Antony found the body of Brutus, wrapped in the best purple garment, burned it, and sent the ashes to his mother, Servilia. Plutarch describes Antony draping his *paludumentum* over the body of Brutus and ordering one of his own freedmen to make arrangements for the burial; after later discovering this man had kept both the *paludumentum* and a good part of the money that should have been spent on the funeral, Antony had him put to death.

Some of those Republicans who made good their escape to Thasos subsequently fled by ship while the others accepted the lead of Messala Corvinus and Cato's grandson Lucius Calpurnius Bibulus in seeking terms from the Triumvirs, surrendering to Antony the significant quantities of money, supplies and war material stored there. Approximately 14,000 Republican legionaries threw down their arms. Besides these the large number of auxiliaries who manned the camps and the surviving redoubts also surrendered.

Rhascus, the Thracian prince, asked for and received as his reward the pardon of his brother, Rhascupolis; according to Appian, this 'made plain that from the beginning these Thracians had not been at variance with each other, but that seeing two great and hostile armies coming into conflict near their territory, they divided the chances of fortune in such a way that the victor might save the vanquished.'

Velleius Paterculus notes that 'No other war cost the blood of so many illustrious men.' The young romantics who had flocked to Brutus's banner in a final burst of Republican idealism were annihilated; the scions of family names to fall in battle included Cato, the only son of Lucullus, the only son of the famed orator Hortensius, and Lucius, the nephew of Cassius. Most of the surviving Republicans immediately transferred their allegiance when a proclamation of amnesty was issued to them, but Caesar's assassins and those who had been proscribed killed themselves or were captured and put to death; among their number, ironically, was Marcus Livius Drusus Claudianus, the father of Livia Drusilla, who later became Octavian's wife. Octavian behaved cruelly to the captives; because of this the rest saluted Antony respectfully as *imperator*, when they were led out in chains, but lashed Octavian to his face with the foulest abuse. Perhaps the last casualty of the battle was Porcia, the wife of Brutus; she perished by her own hand, swallowing the hot embers she snatched from a brazier once news of Philippi arrived in Rome.

The Triumvirs arranged for the demobilization of all their time-expired soldiers, except for 8,000 who volunteered for continued service and were organized into praetorian cohorts to be divided equally between Antony and Octavian. The rest were re-formed, along with the 14,000 Republican legionaries taken captive, into 11 legions. Of these, Antony was to take six, with 10,000 horse, and Octavian five, with 4,000 horse; but as Antony, assuming the mantle of Caesar, had claimed the East as his sphere with the intention of fulfilling the late dictator's abortive campaign against Parthia, Octavian lent him two legions from his quota in return for a promise (subsequently broken) to acquire the two legions Antony had stationed in Italy under Fufius Calenus. The eight legions Antony led east included the VI Ferrata, X Equestris, III Gallica, V Alaudae, and XII Fulminata. Octavian returned to Italy with just three legions, the VII, VIII, and IV Macedonia. Many of the demobilized men were settled at Philippi, which became a Roman colony renamed *Colonia Victrix Philippensium*. Appian sums up the significance of this victory:

> Thus did Octavian and Antony by perilous daring and by two infantry engagements achieve a success, the like of which was never before known; for never before had such numerous and powerful Roman armies come in conflict with each other. These soldiers were not enlisted from the ordinary conscription, but were picked men. They were not new levies, but under long drill and arrayed against each other, not against foreign or barbarous races. Speaking the same language and using the same tactics, being of like discipline and power of endurance, they were for these reasons what we may call

mutually invincible. Nor was there ever such fury and daring in war as here, when citizens contended against citizens, families against families, and fellow-soldiers against each other. The proof of this is that, taking both battles into the account, the number of the slain even among the victors appeared to be not fewer than among the vanquished.

Brunt estimates each side lost 20,000 men during the various engagements of October 42 BC; the Triumvirs alone lost three legions on land and two more at sea on the day of the first battle. Seen purely in terms of lost manpower, Philippi can be considered a disaster to Rome ranking on a par with Cannae and Arausio.

But the outcome at Philippi was a disaster at a deeper level. It was true that scattered embers of resistance to the new regime continued to smoulder. Sextus remained at large, his island fortress of Sicily secure for the moment, and many of the Republican garrisons scattered throughout the east also took to the water, the last refuge from the Triumvirs. Cassius Parmensis, who had been left in Asia with a fleet and an army to collect money, appropriated 30 ships from Rhodes and burned the rest. Clodius, who had been sent by Brutus to Rhodes with 13 ships, found the city in revolt; he evacuated the garrison, some 3,000 men, and joined Parmensis. They were joined by Turulius, who had still more ships under his command. This fleet, which was now quite powerful, manned the ships as best it could with soldiers and with press-ganged slaves, prisoners, and citizens of the islands as rowers. After picking up the refugees from Thasos, including Marcus Cicero, and receiving additional forces under Paulus Aemilius, who had occupied Crete for Brutus, they sailed to the Adriatic where they sided either with Murcus or Ahenobarbus. Murcus joined Sextus with 80 vessels, two legions, 500 archers, and substantial funds; Ahenobarbus, with 70 ships, two legions, and a force of archers and slingers, light-armed troops and gladiators, opted to remain independent; he maintained a guerilla offensive, capturing some of Octavian's ships at Brundisium, burning others, and plundering the surrounding territory.

However, although many Republicans remained at large, the Republican cause itself was lost. The Triumvirs now had more to fear from each other than from any champion of a renascent Republic. But what if Brutus and Cassius had triumphed at Philippi? In the event of the other two-thirds of the Triumvirate being liquidated, there was no possibility of Lepidus being able to prevent the Republicans from reclaiming all Italy and the West. The restoration of legitimate government would be welcomed by a population traumatized by war and proscription. But could it have survived into the Christian era given the endemic structural contradiction inherent in the administrative authority over a multinational empire being monopolized by a parochial urban elite? Only by undertaking the substantial constitutional reform necessary to streamline and liberalize its system of government could the Republic have hoped to meet the obligations of maintaining the *Pax Romana*. Sadly, few of those who fell at Philippi would have accepted this reality; their fundamental motivation was a profoundly conservative allegiance to a way of life that was no longer relevant. If they hadn't given their lives for the Republic of their fathers at Philippi, they, or their heirs, sooner or later would have done so somewhere else.

AFTERMATH

THE WEST: THE PERUSINE WAR

Lucius Antonius was rewarded for his loyalty to his brother with a series of appointments to high office, including tribune of the plebs in 44 BC and consul in 41 BC alongside Publius Servilius Vatia. (Wayne Sayles)

Ironically, the most difficult and dangerous period in the ascendancy of Octavian took place after Philippi. His contribution to the victory when measured against that of Antony left him very much the junior partner; he was so ill during the sojourn back to Rome many despaired of his life; and he was left alone to somehow restore order while simultaneously satisfying a host of mutually irreconcilable interests, a process that spiralled out of control and pushed him to the brink of destruction.

Octavian's top priority upon returning to Italy was to arrange for the settlement of the time-served veterans. Suitable sites had already been designated to provide the necessary allotments and their populations turned out prior to the departure of the Triumvirs for Greece. At least 40 cities, especially in Campania, Samnium, Umbria, Picenum, Etruria, and in northern Italy, were involved in the confiscations.

Each veteran, some 40,000 in all, was allocated up to 40 iugera (25 acres), sufficient for himself and his family. The veterans of XXVI were settled alongside the old Caesarean VII at Luca; Octavian's reconstituted VIII was established at Teanum. Other major cities to be affected included Capua, Beneventum (Benevento), Nuceria (Nocera Inferiore), Venusia (Venosa), Bononia (Bologna), Ancona, and Ariminum (Rimini). Determined to secure for the future the loyalty of the veterans, Octavian rammed through the entire programme within six months. The social dislocation involved has been vividly captured in the works of the poets Virgil and Propertius, whose families lost their property at Mantua and Assisi respectively.

The enforced widespread overnight turnover of landowners massively disrupted the production and distribution of agricultural produce, a process not smoothed by the attitude of the legions, who according to Appian 'encroached upon their neighbours in an insolent manner, seizing more than had been given to them and choosing the best lands.' Many of the dispossessed relocated to Rome, swelling the urban proletariat at the moment the metropolis was struggling to compensate for the impossibility of receiving provisions from Sardinia, Spain, Sicily, and Africa because of the naval blockade imposed by Sextus.

Antony's representatives in Rome sought, without his authorization, to take advantage of this upheaval by channelling the public anger against Octavian. Ostensibly, this power play was headed by Antony's brother, Lucius, one of the consuls for 41 BC, but the prime mover was in fact Antony's

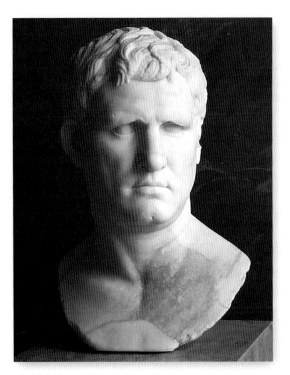

Already a close confidant of his childhood friend Octavian, Marcus Vipsanius Agrippa, depicted here in a bust held in the Borghese Collection, the Louvre, began to come into his own as a field commander during the Perusine War. After the treachery of Salvidienus his position at the right hand of Octavian was secure.

wife (and Octavian's mother-in-law) Fulvia, who, according to Velleius Paterculus, 'had nothing of the woman in her except her sex.' The Antonians fanned the flames of resentment among those alienated by Octavian's misrule; Republican diehards who still refused to accept the new order, non-Latin provincials exasperated by Roman high-handedness, and above all, those dispossessed by the settlement of the veterans. The regions where what became known as the Perusine War was fought correspond almost perfectly to those where the confiscations took place.

Octavian's authority rested on a single pillar, the support of the veterans. This severely restricted his capacity to make the concessions over the land distribution necessary to defuse the increasing tension. His attempts to conciliate local opinion by limiting the transfer of ownership backfired because the veterans were convinced that Octavian's compromises were at their expense. According to Dio, they killed many of the centurions and others who were loyal to Octavian and were trying to restrain them from rioting, and they came very near to slaying Octavian himself.

Armed resistance to the regime broke out in a bush-fire fashion across Italy. Octavian marched against the Sabine city of Nursia (Norcia) but was repulsed by Tisienus Gallus. He then targeted the Umbrian city of Sentinum but again was thwarted, this time by Gaius Furnius.

While Octavian was thus engaged Lucius, after sending three cohorts ahead, which slipped into the city clandestinely by night, marched on Rome, drove off the cavalry force that met him, and took the city, the soldiers who had already arrived there joining in the assault. Lepidus fled to Octavian, who left Quintus Salvidienus Rufus to maintain the siege of Sentinum and set out for Rome. When Furnius sallied forth in pursuit, leaving the city vulnerable, Salvidienus plundered and burned it.

Lucius abandoned Rome at Octavian's approach and headed northwards, hoping to effect a junction with Ventidius and Pollio. Salvidienus, who had been ordered into Spain earlier in the year, was recalled by Octavian, and made his way back to Italy through Gallia Cisalpina while being shadowed by Pollio and Ventidius.

Lucius occupied Perusia (Perugia), a city on a ridge at the north-west end of the great Umbrian plain, with six legions. He expected to appeal to the local population, some of whom had been dispossessed of their farms by the colonists at nearby Hispellum, and for the substantial Antonian forces under Pollio and Ventidius to march to his relief. Accordingly, he only provisioned the city to withstand a brief siege.

Immediately upon his arrival Octavian drew a palisade and ditch around Perusia 10km in circuit, extending long arms to the Tiber so that nothing could slip through into the city. Lucius responded by sending a force of 4,000 horse to pillage Octavian's supplies in order to force him to raise the siege. Fulvia meanwhile gathered reinforcements, which she sent to Lucius under Plancus, who en route intercepted and destroyed one of Octavian's legions while it was on the march to Rome.

LEFT
The Etruscan Arch in the city wall of Perusia, modern Perugia. Along with the temples of Vulcan and Juno these walls were the only structures to survive the inferno that consumed the city at the end of the seven-week siege in 40 BC. (Courtesy Milko Anselmi)

BELOW LEFT
A close-up of the Etruscan Arch; note the retrospective salutation to the conqueror of the city through the incorporation of his name in its title. (Courtesy Milko Anselmi)

Pollio and Ventidius marched south but halted and then retreated when confronted by Agrippa, Pollio retiring to Ravenna, Ventidius to Ariminum. Plancus advanced no further than Spoletium (Spoleto). Octavian stationed a force in front of each, to prevent them from coalescing, and tightened his blockade of Perusia, expanding the depth and width of his ditch to 9m and increasing the height of his wall, constructing 1,500 wooden towers on it, 18m apart. While these works were under construction there were frequent sorties and skirmishes, but the real enemy to both sides was hunger. The question was which side would break first; Perusia was slowly being reduced by famine but the people of Rome were suffering too; they openly denounced the war and civil disobedience was escalating.

The Italian theatre of operations, 44–38 BC

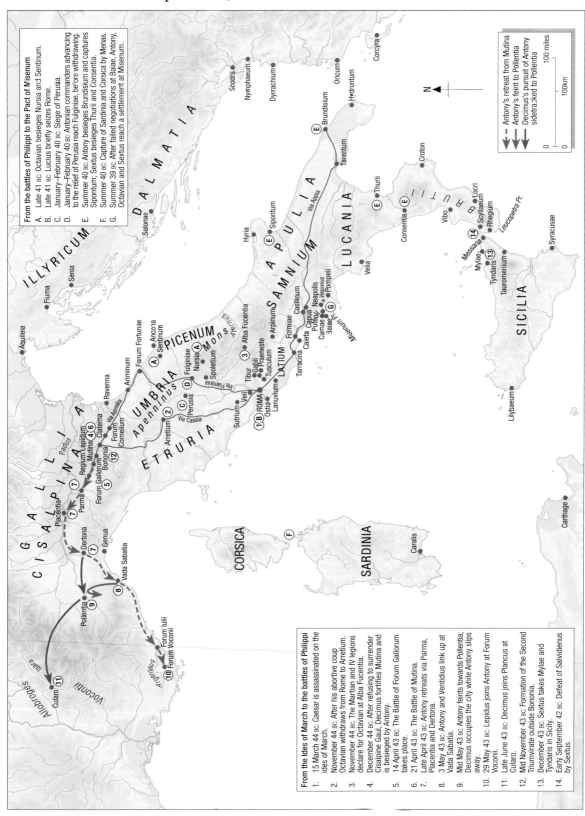

- - → Antony's retreat from Mutina
⬇ Antony's feint to Pollentia
⬇ Decimus's pursuit of Antony sidetracked to Pollentia

0   100 miles
0   100km

The Antonian commanders finally linked up and advanced, to the relief of Lucius. At Fulginiae (Foligno), less than 30km from Perusia, where their signal fires could be seen, they encountered Agrippa and Salvidienus. Ventidius and Pollio wanted to fight, but Plancus wanted to await events and, unable to arrive at a consensus in favour of battle, the Antonians withdrew, abandoning Perusia to its fate. Those in the city who had rejoiced when they saw the fires assumed the worst when the signals ceased. After a night assault extending from the first watch until daylight around the whole circumvallation failed, Lucius took an account of the remaining provisions, forbade giving any to the slaves, and prohibited them from escaping to prevent the enemy becoming aware of just how desperate his situation was. The slaves were reduced to eating grass or green leaves wherever they could find them; those who died were buried in mass graves.

Lucius made one last attempt to break the siege, which failed; out of options, he finally surrendered. His life was spared, but many of the leading citizens of Perusia were executed and the city itself went up in flames.

The Antonian commanders had failed to intervene, despite having concentrated 13 veteran legions and 6,500 horse at Fulginiae, because they could not resolve a double problem; they had received no instruction from Antony regarding how to proceed, and they couldn't trust the men under their command. Every legionary under arms aspired to own a plot of land upon being mustered out and Octavian was attempting to fulfil this aspiration for tens of thousands of their comrades. Would the legions march against him?

The politicization of the veterans had been demonstrated at the threshold of the war when they assembled on the Capitol in great numbers and after commanding that the compact between Antony and Octavian following Philippi be read to them, they ratified these agreements and voted that they themselves should be made arbitrators of the differences between them. After recording this action on tablets and sealing them, they delivered them to the Vestal Virgins to keep; and they ordered Octavian, who was present, and Lucius through an embassy, to present themselves for arbitration at Gabii, a city midway between Rome and Praeneste (Palestrina), on a stated day. A council-chamber was prepared with platforms for the speakers in the centre, as in a regular trial. Octavian submitted in person to this mediation but his rivals did not; the veterans accordingly condemned Lucius and Fulvia as the guilty parties and espoused the cause of Octavian.

Such wilful independence also accounts for Antony's passivity throughout the crisis. He could not denounce his wife and brother for defending his interests, but openly siding with them risked alienating the legions. The only safe option was silence.

The surrender of Perusia did not precipitate the collapse of the Antonian cause; only two legions belonging to Plancus, which were intercepted at

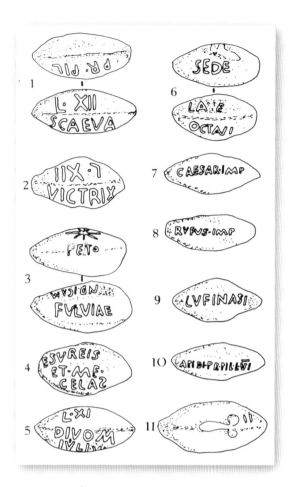

A reconstruction of lead slingbolts recovered from archaeological surveys at Perugia. The missiles flung by both besiegers and besieged incorporate text and images ranging from unit identification markers to scatological insults intended for the enemy. (Courtesy Lawrence Keppie)

This coin was issued to celebrate the union of Antony and Octavian's sister Octavia. This political match resolved the Perusine War and succeeded in postponing a final reckoning between the Triumvirs for another eight years. (Wayne Sayles)

Cameria, were persuaded by Agrippa to desert to him. Fulvia fled with her children and 3,000 horse to Dicaearchia and then Brundisium. She put to sea, accompanied by Plancus, who had abandoned the remnant of his army, which elected to serve under Ventidius. From Ravenna, Pollio joined Ahenobarbus, who was in control of the Adriatic, inducing him to join the Antonians.

Antony was less than enthusiastic about the news Fulvia brought him when they met in Athens; he upbraided her severely for acting so recklessly on his behalf without his authority. He was no doubt more relieved to greet his mother Julia, who had fled to Sextus, where she was received with great kindness. Sextus sent her and an embassy to Antony, bearing with them the proposal of an alliance. Antony thanked Sextus for sending his mother and informed his ambassadors that if there should be a war with Octavian he would ally himself with Sextus, but if Octavian should adhere to their agreements he would endeavour to reconcile him with Sextus. Another to find refuge with Sextus was Tiberius Claudius Nero, who had commanded a garrison in Campania for the Antonians before being forced to flee with his wife Livia and son Tiberius – the future wife and heir of Octavian, respectively.

Antony could no longer risk allowing Octavian to assume absolute power in Rome. With no option but to defend his interests in person he left Fulvia ill at Sicyon and set sail from Corcyra. The problem was that, with his forces in the East having melted away before the Parthian onslaught, he brought with him little more than the praetorian cohort that had accompanied him to Alexandria. He rendezvoused with Ahenobarbus at sea and picked up the erstwhile Republican's army at Paloeis. The combined force sailed to Brundisium, which was garrisoned by five cohorts of Octavian's troops. The citizens closed their gates against Ahenobarbus, as an old enemy, and against Antony, as one introducing an enemy. Antony, indignantly assuming he was in fact shut out by the garrison on Octavian's orders, drew a ditch and palisade across the isthmus that connected the town to the mainland. Antony also surrounded the harbour and the islands in it with towers planted closely together and sent additional forces along the coasts of Italy to seize the advantageous positions.

Antony widened the war by calling on Sextus to move against Octavian. In a desperate bid to neutralize Sextus, Octavian had divorced Fulvia's daughter Clodia and married Scribonia, the sister of Lucius Libo, the father-in-law of Sextus. This did not deter Sextus from dispatching Menas with four legions to take Sardinia. Menas seized the provincial capital, Caralis, and incorporated the two resident legions into his army. At some point Sextus also occupied Corsica. In Italy, Antony captured the town of Sipontum in Ausonia while Sextus besieged Thurii in Lucania and Consentia (Cosenza) in Bruttium, ravaging their territory with his cavalry.

Octavian was beset on all sides. In Africa, Sextius, an ally of Antony, had just handed over his command to Fuficius Fango, a partisan of Octavian. On the authority of Lucius, Sextius collected a force composed of retired veterans and a miscellaneous crowd of Africans, including auxiliaries of the native princes, and entered the war. Fango, having been defeated on both wings in pitched battle and having lost his camp, was driven into the hills on the frontier where, mistaking the rushing of a troop of wild buffaloes for a night attack of Numidian horse, he committed suicide. Farther west, the co-rulers of Mauretania squabbled; at the instigation of Lucius, King Bogud invaded Spain only to lose his half of the kingdom to his brother King Bocchus II, who supported Octavian.

Antony convened an assembly of the subject client states here at Ephesus, the greatest city in Asia Minor, after assuming command of the East. (Author's collection)

The turning point, which constituted a significant advantage for Octavian but at the same time threatened to drive his relations with Antony into open war, was the death of Quintus Fufius Calenus in Cisalpine Gaul with the consequent transfer of his 11 legions to Octavian.

Now Octavian was in a position to take the initiative. He sent Agrippa into Ausonia, where he took Sipontum by storm, calling out the colonized veterans en route. Assuming they were being mobilized against Sextus they fell into line but upon discovering they were being led against Antony they dispersed back to their homes. Octavian, while marching to Brundisium with another army, fell in with these men and prevailed upon those he had colonized to follow him. They did so, but with the secret intention of reconciling Octavian with Antony; only if Antony should refuse and go to war would they fight for Octavian.

Although his forces enjoyed an enormous numerical superiority, Octavian could do nothing but encamp adjacent to Brundisium upon his arrival and await events because he could not trust that his men would take the field against Antony. Antony summoned the army of Marcius Censorinus, whom he had appointed governor of Macedonia; in the meantime, he resorted to the stratagem of sending warships and merchant vessels to sea by night secretly with a multitude of private citizens on board, who returned, in batches, the next day, in sight of Octavian, fully armed, as though they had just come from Macedonia.

Antony was about to attack Brundisium when he was informed Publius Servilius Rullus was coming to the assistance of Octavian with 1,500 horse. According to Appian, Antony could not restrain his rage, but sprang up from his meal and, with such friends as he could find ready and with 400 horse, he pressed forwards, and fell upon the 1,500, who were still asleep near the town of Hyria, threw them into a panic, captured them without a fight, and returned to Brundisium the same day. As Appian notes, 'Thus did the reputation that Antony had gained at Philippi as invincible still inspire terror.'

Before the stalemate could be broken the news arrived that Fulvia had died in Sicyon, where her husband had abandoned her; According to Appian, 'Antony was much saddened by this event because he considered himself in

some sense the cause of it.' Nevertheless, the death of Fulvia afforded the pretext to begin negotiations. Antony signalled he was ready to talk by sending Sextus back to Sicily with nothing more concrete than a pledge to represent their mutual concerns, and ordering Ahenobarbus to quit the theatre altogether and take office as governor of Bithynia. When Octavian's veterans learned these facts they chose representatives and sent them to both commanders in order to hammer out an agreement.

As finally adjudicated by Gaius Maecenas for Octavian, Pollio for Antony, and their mutual friend Lucius Cocceius Nerva, under the terms of the Pact of Brundisium the estranged Triumvirs would divide the Roman world between them. Octavian would take the West, Antony the East; the River Drin, the boundary between the provinces of Illyricum and Macedonia, would serve as their frontier. Each man would have an equal share in levying troops from Italy. To seal the arrangement, Antony took Octavian's recently widowed sister Octavia as his wife, the Senate dispensing with the law by which a widow was not permitted to marry until 10 months after the death of her husband.

Lucius was appointed governor of Spain where shortly after taking command he conveniently, though none of the sources suggest suspiciously, died. Octavian also sent Lepidus with six legions to take the helm in Africa, where Sextius was obliged to surrender the four legions under his command.

Octavian replaced Pollio with Alfenus Varus in Gallia Cisalpina and sent Salvidienus to Gallia Narbonensis. Although he had been promised the consulship, Salvidienus wrote to Antony offering to induce the troops in his province to desert from Octavian. His proposal could not have been more poorly timed; to demonstrate his commitment to their renewed partnership, Antony revealed to Octavian the treachery of Salvidienus, who was arraigned for treason before the Senate and condemned to death.

Rome rejoiced at the reconciliation of Antony and Octavian but groaned at the ongoing depredations of Sextus, who not only blockaded the city but raided her ports, Puteoli and Ostia. The populace held the Triumvirs responsible for prolonging the war and made their opinion clear on such public occasions as the games in the Circus, when they honoured by loud applause the statue of Neptune when it was displayed, Sextus having styled himself the son of the sea god. In this atmosphere the imposition of another round of taxation and requisitioning by the Triumvirs in order to fund a fresh campaign against Sextus provoked a riot. Octavian with only a handful of praetorians went to the forum to intercede with the mob, but as soon as he

Prince Pacorus of Parthia, son of Orodes II and brother-in-law of King Artavasdes II of Armenia. In the name of his father he twice led incursions into Roman territory, but was out-matched tactically on both occasions – after Carrhae by Cassius and after Philippi by Ventidius. (CNG)

made his appearance he was subjected to a barrage of curses and stones. He escaped with his life only because Antony summoned troops from outside the city and, amidst terrible scenes of panic in the crowded streets, hacked his way into the forum to rescue his junior colleague. After the mob was dispersed the corpses were thrown into the Tiber in order to spare the city their gruesome appearance. But it was clear the Triumvirs had no option but to open negotiations.

Sextus's heterogeneous inner circle was divided over whether to continue to resist the reconstituted Triumvirate and was riven with internal jealousies; on the advice of Menas, Sextus had his rival Murcus murdered. In their first meeting on the coast at Baiae (Baia), Sextus and the Triumvirs attempted to, literally, meet in the middle, Antony and Octavian building a platform extending from the land out to sea, Sextus constructing one to shore from his ships. When it was made clear to Sextus his ambition to replace Lepidus in the Triumvirate would not be realized he broke off negotiations.

Talks resumed at Misenum. This time the Triumvirs took their station on the shore and Sextus on a mound that had been constructed in the sea. The terms finally agreed to were that Sextus had to withdraw his troops from Italy, discontinue his raids, and supply Rome with grain. In return, he would govern Sicily, Sardinia, Corsica, and the Peloponnesus, would be made augur and later consul *in absentia*, and would be compensated for the loss of his patrimony. All the exiles with him (except the assassins of Caesar) would be restored to citizenship and a quarter of their property remitted; slaves who had fled to him would remain free.

Octavian must have reflected on two key lessons from the Perusine War; first, that the general populace was crying out for peace after ten years of civil strife; and second, that the legions would not fight Antony, who they still respected as the first man in Rome. Fortunately, in this instance his youth was on his side; he could afford to postpone the final reckoning until old scars had healed and old allegiances faded.

THE EAST: THE PARTHIAN INTERVENTION

After Philippi, Antony had crossed into Asia to pacify and reorganize the East. At Ephesus he convened an assembly of the various subject provinces and cities in order to more effectively squeeze out of them whatever capital they had left after the exactions of Brutus and Cassius. He then made a grand

This remarkable coin issued by Quintus Labienus hails him as 'Parthicus Imp' – as though he had earned the accolade of *imperator* in action against the Parthians, instead of at the head of their army. (Wayne Sayles)

tour through Asia Minor, Syria and Palestine, arranging political and economic affairs, installing loyalists in key positions of authority, including Saxa as governor of Syria, Plancus as governor of Asia, and Publius Canidius Crassus as his representative in the client state of Armenia.

While at Tarsus, Antony summoned Cleopatra to account for her failure to aid the Triumvirs in the struggle against the Republicans. Her arrival, borne up the Cydnus River on an ornamental barge, changed the course of history; not only did Antony accept her justifications for non-intervention during the late war he liquidated her political rivals and then accompanied her back to Alexandria in the winter of 41/40 BC; twins, Alexander Helios and Cleopatra Selene, were the fruit of this interlude.

While Antony was indulging himself in Egypt a significant new threat was rising to the east. Quintus Labienus, the son of Caesar's trusted right-hand man turned arch enemy Titus Labienus, had been posted by Brutus and Cassius as their representative at the court of Orodes II of Parthia. In the wake of Philippi he remained in Ctesiphon where he was able to convince the king that the state of flux within the republic made this the ideal time for Parthia to strike. In early 40 BC Labienus and the king's son, Prince Pacorus, crossed the Euphrates with a powerful force and struck at Apamea. They were repulsed from the city, but, as he had promised, Labienus was able to win over the garrisons stationed in the country to his side without resistance, for these largely consisted of troops that had served with Brutus and Cassius; Antony had incorporated them into his own forces and had assigned them to garrison Syria because they knew the country.

Labienus then defeated Saxa in a pitched battle, 'through the superior numbers and ability of his cavalry,' Dio notes. Saxa withdrew but, afraid his men would turn on him – Labienus was trying to lure them away by means of pamphlets which he kept shooting into Saxa's camp – he fled towards Cilicia, only to be captured and put to death en route. Apamea surrendered, followed by Antioch. The two Parthian commanders then divided their forces. Pacorus went south and quickly rolled up all of Syria, Phoenicia and Judea bar Tyre, which he could not besiege because he had no fleet.

Labienus occupied Cilicia and marched into Anatolia, taking control of the entire peninsula while Plancus, his troops melting away, fled to the Aegean islands. The only city on the mainland to hold out was Stratonicea, which withstood a long siege. Most cities surrendered without resistance, but Mylasa and Alabanda rose up against their garrisons. Strabo relates that it was the orator Hybreas who inspired the people of Mylasa to rebel, having already earned the ire of Labienus, for when he proclaimed himself Parthian Emperor, Hybreas responded: 'Then I too call myself Carian Emperor.' Labienus, unamused, razed the city to the ground when he recaptured it; surviving bureaucratic commentary from later in the decade confirms the city had still not fully recovered 'from the ruin that came from the looting of Labienus.'

In less than a year the Parthians had re-established Persian authority at nearly the limits of the old Achaemenid Empire. Antony had to respond. He departed Alexandria (he would not lay eyes on Cleopatra for the next four years) and first went to Tyre and then Cyprus, Rhodes and Asia Minor, gathering his fleet and troops. But his preparations were disrupted by the news of the crisis developing in the west. It was only after returning to Italy and securing his political base at Rome that he was able to focus on eastern matters, and he did so not in person but by dispatching Ventidius in his place.

Early in 39 BC Ventidius and his legate Popaedius Silo embarked for the East with 11 legions and a strong force of slingers. Ventidius attacked Labienus immediately after landing in Asia Minor and before Labienus knew he had arrived. Caught off guard with only a small body of troops Labienus was forced to retreat into Syria, where he received Parthian reinforcements. Ventidius finally overtook him on the Syrian slope of the Taurus Mountains. Although Ventidius remained on high ground the overconfident Parthian cataphracts did not wait for Labienus but charged uphill at dawn to destroy the Romans. Ventidius held his men in check until all the Parthians were on the steep slope. Then he gave his legions the order to launch their *pila* and charge under the cover of a hail of lead from the Roman slingers. The cataphracts were routed, fleeing into Cilicia. Labienus was killed trying to escape; most of his forces joined Ventidius's army.

The retreating Parthians under Pharnastanes took a stand at the Amanus Gates at the border between Syria and Cilicia. Ventidius posted 18 cohorts at the side of his camp in a hidden valley, with cavalry stationed behind the infantry. Then he sent Silo on ahead with a small force to lure the Parthians from their strong position. The Parthians, in hot pursuit of the fleeing Roman cavalry, were hit on their flanks and slaughtered, Pharnastanes among them. Having secured Cilicia, Ventidius recovered Syria without fighting a battle, for Pacorus evidently withdrew from the province late in 39 BC. Ventidius went on to occupy Judea without difficulty before the end of the year.

Early in the spring of 38 BC, while the legions of Ventidius were still strung out in winter quarters from Judaea to Cappadocia, Pacorus again invaded Syria. In order to gain time to gather his scattered forces Ventidius resorted to a clever subterfuge. He knew that Prince Pharnaeus of Cyrrhestica, who pretended to be a Roman ally, was in reality loyal to Parthia. He pretended to confide in Pharnaeus that he was concerned the Parthians might forsake the place where they usually crossed the Euphrates, near the town of Zeugma, and use some other crossing farther downstream; for this territory was a plain, ideal terrain for the Persian cavalry, whereas the crossing at Zeugma was over a deep stream, and the terrain was rugged, affording the Roman troops protection from the Parthian archers.

More than a century before the Sicarii made their epic last stand at Masada, Herod was forced to take refuge on its heights after the Parthians installed his rival Antigonus on the throne of Jerusalem. (Author's collection)

After escaping to Rome and being recognized as 'King of the Jews' by the Senate, Herod returned to Judea, sealing his victory in the ensuing civil war with the conquest of Jerusalem (depicted in this late-15th-century painting by Jean Fouquet) and the crucifixion of Antigonus – not the first time, and far from the last, that the holy city would be profaned by war and murder.

Pharnaeus was deceived and relayed the disinformation to Pacorus. The Parthian leader, responding to this supposed intelligence coup, avoided the short route by Zeugma, and led his troops by the long route through Cyrrhestica. Furthermore, Pacorus wasted 40 days gathering materials and constructing a bridge across the Euphrates.

Ventidius utilized the time he had gained by this stratagem to consolidate his forces and was ready for action in Cyrrhestica three days before the arrival of Pacorus. The Parthians found their crossing unopposed and when the Romans did not take the initiative but remained on high ground Pacorus became overconfident and boldly attacked the fortified Roman camp. Ventidius kept his men in check until the Parthians were within 500 paces before ordering a sally that drove the Parthian cavalry down the hill in confusion. At the foot of the hill the cataphracts made a valiant stand, but when Pacorus was slain most of them fled, although a handful fought vainly to the death while attempting to save his body.

The death of Pacorus and the destruction of his army was regarded by the Romans as a victory that went far to redeem the disgrace of Carrhae. Ventidius maximized the political capital of his victory by sending Pacorus's head for prominent display in the disaffected cities of the East, but since some of Pacorus's fugitive Parthians had taken refuge with Antiochus of Commagene, Ventidius moved against Samosata. Plutarch says Antiochus offered 1,000 talents to secure a pardon, but Antony, who was finally on the march, told Ventidius to make no terms with Antiochus, then summarily relieved him of command. The jealous Triumvir then settled with Antiochus for 300 talents after an unsuccessful siege.

There was one last spasm of violence before the East was finally pacified. In 43 BC Antigonus, the son of Aristobulus II, the last king of Judea, tried to seize the throne from his uncle, the Ethnarch Hyrcanus II. He was defeated by the governor of Galilee, Herod. In 40 BC Antigonus tried to take the throne again and on this occasion, with the aid of Pacorus, he was successful, seizing Jerusalem and mutilating his uncle so he could no longer serve as high priest, a title Antigonus usurped, along with that of king. Herod took refuge in the citadel of Masada before seeking support in Rome, where he was elected King of the Jews by the Senate in 39 BC. Upon returning to Judea he waged war against Antigonus for two years until he was finally able to lay siege to Jerusalem in the spring of 37 BC aided by a Roman commitment under Gaius Sosius of 11 legions, 6,000 cavalry and auxiliary troops to supplement his own 30,000-strong force. In the summer, Herod at last took the city and executed Antigonus. He would be recognized as the sole ruler of Judea for the next 34 years and prove a loyal ally to Antony, though by no means his closest confidant. That role was usurped by Cleopatra, and her influence would precipitate the final conflict that would define the form of the autocracy destined to supersede the republic of Rome.

The eastern theatre of operations, 44–38 BC

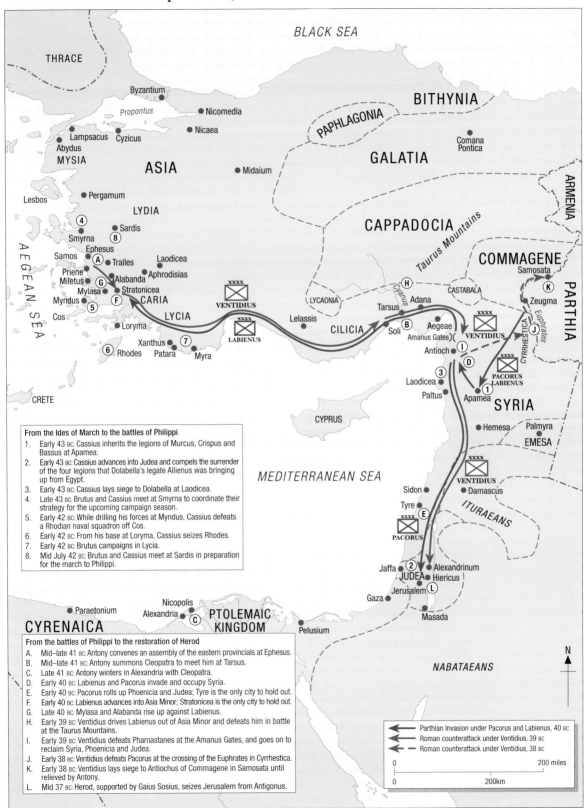

BLACK SEA

THRACE

Byzantium

Propontis

Nicomedia

Nicaea

BITHYNIA

PAPHLAGONIA

GALATIA

Comana
Pontica

ARMENIA

Lampsacus
Abydus
Cyzicus

MYSIA

ASIA

Midaium

Lesbos

Pergamum

LYDIA

④
⑧

Sardis

Smyrna

Ephesus

Samos

Ⓐ Tralles

Laodicea

Priene
Miletus
Ⓖ Alabanda

Aphrodisias

Mylasa Ⓕ Stratonicea

CARIA

Myndus

⑤

Cos

LYCIA

Loryma

Xanthus ⑦
⑥ Rhodes Patara
Myra

CAPPADOCIA

Taurus Mountains

COMMAGENE

Samosata

Ⓚ

PARTHIA

Cydnus

Ⓗ

CASTABALA

Zeugma

Ⓙ

CYRRHESTICA

Euphrates

XXXX
VENTIDIUS

LYCAONIA

Lelassis

CILICIA

Tarsus

Adana

Soli Ⓑ Aegeae

Amanus Gates

XXXX
VENTIDIUS

XXXX
PACORUS
LABIENUS

XXXX
LABIENUS

AEGEAN SEA

Ⓘ

Antioch

Ⓓ

①

Apamea

SYRIA

CRETE

Laodicea ③
Paltus

CYPRUS

Hemesa

Palmyra

EMESA

MEDITERRANEAN SEA

Sidon

XXXX
VENTIDIUS

Damascus

ITURAEANS

Tyre

Ⓔ

XXXX
PACORUS

Jaffa ②
JUDEA Ⓛ
Jerusalem

Gaza

Alexandrinum
Hiericus

Masada

N

From the Ides of March to the battles of Philippi

1. Early 43 BC: Cassius inherits the legions of Murcus, Crispus and Bassus at Apamea.
2. Early 43 BC: Cassius advances into Judea and compels the surrender of the four legions that Dolabella's legate Allienus was bringing up from Egypt.
3. Early 43 BC: Cassius lays siege to Dolabella at Laodicea.
4. Late 43 BC: Brutus and Cassius meet at Smyrna to coordinate their strategy for the upcoming campaign season.
5. Early 42 BC: While drilling his forces at Myndus, Cassius defeats a Rhodian naval squadron off Cos.
6. Early 42 BC: From his base at Loryma, Cassius seizes Rhodes.
7. Early 42 BC: Brutus campaigns in Lycia.
8. Mid July 42 BC: Brutus and Cassius meet at Sardis in preparation for the march to Philippi.

Paraetonium

Nicopolis
Alexandria Ⓒ PTOLEMAIC
KINGDOM

CYRENAICA

Pelusium

NABATAEANS

From the battles of Philippi to the restoration of Herod

A. Mid–late 41 BC: Antony convenes an assembly of the eastern provincials at Ephesus.
B. Mid–late 41 BC: Antony summons Cleopatra to meet him at Tarsus.
C. Late 41 BC: Antony winters in Alexandria with Cleopatra.
D. Early 40 BC: Labienus and Pacorus invade and occupy Syria.
E. Early 40 BC: Pacorus rolls up Phoenicia and Judea; Tyre is the only city to hold out.
F. Early 40 BC: Labienus advances into Asia Minor; Stratonicea is the only city to hold out.
G. Late 40 BC: Mylasa and Alabanda rise up against Labienus.
H. Early 39 BC: Ventidius drives Labienus out of Asia Minor and defeats him in battle at the Taurus Mountains.
I. Early 39 BC: Ventidius defeats Pharnastanes at the Amanus Gates, and goes on to reclaim Syria, Phoenicia and Judea.
J. Early 38 BC: Ventidius defeats Pacorus at the crossing of the Euphrates in Cyrrhestica.
K. Early 38 BC: Ventidius lays siege to Antiochus of Commagene in Samosata until relieved by Antony.
L. Mid 37 BC: Herod, supported by Gaius Sosius, seizes Jerusalem from Antigonus.

Parthian Invasion under Pacorus and Labienus, 40 BC
Roman counterattack under Ventidius, 39 BC
Roman counterattack under Ventidius, 38 BC

0   200 miles
0   200km

THE BATTLEFIELD TODAY

The gateway to Philippi is the modern city of Kavala (a.k.a. the republican port of Neapolis), which sits athwart the main highway linking Macedonia with Thrace (roughly nine to ten hours from Athens by KTEL coach) but has no rail link. Kavala does boast an international airport, the rather grandiloquently titled 'Megas Alexandros' (KVA), at Chrisoupoli, 33km from the city centre, which is a hub for a regular shuttle service by the domestic carriers Aegean and Olympic. As Kavala has been a major port since the 6th century BC perhaps the most pleasant means of arrival is by sea.

The easiest way to get to Philippi is to catch one of the commuter buses heading north to Krinidhes (the town adjacent to the site) on a regular basis – just ask the driver to drop you off at the site, which is about €2 and 15 km from Kavala's downtown depot. The best time of year to explore Philippi is summer, when the site is open 8am to 7.30pm daily. Full admission is €3. The bus route bisects the site and is extremely busy, so choose your moment to cross from one side to the other carefully. It's best to start on the east side and climb to the top of the acropolis; from there you can get your bearings. Directly to the west are the ruins of the agora. Settled by discharged veterans after the battle, Philippi flourished until being reduced to a bone of contention between Byzantines, Bulgars and Serbs led to its being abandoned during the Middle Ages. Many Christian tour groups visit the site as Philippi was home to the first Christian community in Europe; it was visited in antiquity by the Apostle Paul, who preached and was imprisoned here on his first visit in AD 49 or 50 (the so-called 'prison of the Apostle Paul' on the site is in fact a Roman water cistern which was later converted into a cult place). Paul made two subsequent visits, in AD 56 and 57.

Located north-west and south-west from the summit of the acropolis are the slopes where Brutus and Cassius fortified their camps; in the distance directly to the west is the site of the Triumvirs' camp. The landscape has changed significantly over the past two millennia. Most significantly, the swamp that dominated the region even at the end of the 19th century has been entirely converted into farmland, so the mind's eye has to imagine Antony's legions emerging from the morass and swarming against the Republican army at the base of the high ground. No physical traces of the battle have been recovered, meaning the evocative words of the poet Virgil, in ending the first book of his *Georgics*, have yet to be realized: 'Surely also a time will come, when in these lands a farmer, laboriously plowing the ground will find Roman spears eaten away by flaking rust, or will strike empty helmets with his heavy hoes.'

BIBLIOGRAPHY

We don't have Caesar's magisterial, pseudo-detached commentary for this campaign as we did for Pharsalus so the only extant contemporary source are the letters of Cicero until they are so abruptly cut off. What happened subsequent to the ides of March has been reconstructed largely from the histories of Appian and Cassius Dio, the relevant chapters of Plutarch and Suetonius, and whatever else can be gleaned from the fragments of other authors that have survived antiquity, including Frontinus, Vegetius, and Velleius Paterculus.

The best recent overview of the period is Osgood, Josiah, *Caesar's Legacy: Civil War and the Emergence of the Roman Empire*, Cambridge University Press, Cambridge, 2006. Other useful titles include Gowing, Alain M., *The Triumviral Narratives of Appian and Cassius Dio*, University of Michigan Press, Ann Arbor, 1992; Cook, S.A., Adcock, M.A., and Charlesworth, M.P., *The Cambridge Ancient History Vol. X: The Augustan Empire, 44 BC–AD 70*, Cambridge University Press, Cambridge, 1979; Syme, Ronald, *The Roman Revolution*, Oxford University Press, Oxford, 1960; Holmes, T. Rice, *The Architect of the Roman Empire*, Oxford University Press, New York, 1928; and Ferrero, Guglielmo, *The Greatness and Decline of Rome, Vol. III: The Fall of an Aristocracy*, Putnam, New York, 1909.

Many accounts of the post-Caesarean era incorporate biographies of the key players in the fall of the Republic. On the Triumvirs' side, Mark Antony is studied in Huzar, Eleanor, *Marc Antony: A Biography*, University of Minnesota Press, Minneapolis, 1978; Roberts, Alan, *Mark Antony: His Life and Times*, Malvern Publishing, Upton-Upon-Severn, 1988; and Weigall, Arthur, *The Life and Times of Marc Anthony*, Putnam's, New York, 1931. The career of his wilful wife Fulvia is assessed by Delia, Diana, 'Fulvia Reconsidered' in Pomeroy, Sarah B., *Women's History and Ancient History*, University of North Carolina Press, Chapel Hill, 1991, pp. 197–217. For the junior partner in the Triumvirate see Weigel, Richard D., *Lepidus: The Tarnished Triumvir*, Routledge, New York, 1992.

For the Republicans, a good short overview of the characters of Brutus and Cassius is Rawson, Elizabeth, 'Cassius and Brutus: The Memory of the Liberators,' in Moxon, I.S., Smart, J.D., and Woodman, A.J. (eds.), *Past Perspectives: Studies in Greek and Roman Historical Writing*, Cambridge University Press, Cambridge, 1986, pp. 101–119. The twilight of Cicero's career is covered in Lacey, W.K., *Cicero and the End of the Roman Republic*, Barnes & Noble Books, New York, 1978. For the role of Sextus Pompey see Powell, Anton and Welch, Kathryn (eds.), *Sextus Pompeius*, Classical Press of Wales, Swansea, 2002, and Hadas, Moses, *Sextus Pompey*, AMS Press, New York, 1966.

Titles focusing on the military formations, weapons, and tactics of the late Republic include

The enduring fascination of the fall of the Roman Republic, when, according to Dio, 'as never before liberty and popular government were the issues of the struggle,' continues to resonate in the popular imagination. One example is Shakespeare's epic interpretation, *Julius Caesar*, which attracts major talent in both stage and screen productions – the role of Antony having been played by Marlon Brando and Charlton Heston, while Denzel Washington played Brutus in a recent revival on Broadway. (Playbill)

Brunt, P.A., *Italian Manpower 25 B.C. – A.D. 14*, Clarendon Press, Oxford, 1971, esp. Chapter XXVI, 'Men Under Arms, 49–29 B.C.,' pp. 473–512 (complemented by lo Cascio, Elio, 'Recruitment and the Size of the Roman Population from the Third to the First Century BCE,' in Scheidel, Walter (ed.), *Debating Roman Demography*, Brill, Boston, 2001, pp. 111–138); Keppie, Lawrence, *The Making of the Roman Army: From Republic to Empire*, University of Oklahoma Press, Norman, 1984, esp. Chapter 4, 'Civil War,' pp. 103–131; Grant, Michael, *The Army of the Caesars*, Scribner's, New York, 1974, esp. Chapter 1, 'Army Leadership in the Failing Republic 107–31 BC,' pp. 3–35; and the trilogy Goldsworthy, Adrian, *The Complete Roman Army*, Thames & Hudson, London, 2003, Goldsworthy, Adrian, *Roman Warfare*, Cassell, London, 2000, and Goldsworthy, Adrian, *The Roman Army at War, 100 BC–AD 200*, Clarendon Press, Oxford, 1996. See also Botermann, Helga, *Die Soldaten und die Römische Republik in der Zeit von Caesars Tod bis zur Begründung des Zweiten Triumvirats*, Beck, Munich, 1968, and 'The Legion as Society,' Chapter 22 in MacMullen, Ramsay, *Changes in the Roman Empire*, Princeton University Press, Princeton, 1990, pp. 225–235.

Some excellent recent scholarship on the nature of combat includes Cowan, Ross, *Roman Legionary 58 BC – AD 69*, Osprey Publishing, Oxford, 2003; Cowan, Ross, 'The Clashing of Weapons and Silent Advances in Roman Battles,' Historia, Vol. 56, No. 1, 2007, pp. 114–117; Sabin, Philip, 'The Face of Roman Battle,' *The Journal of Roman Studies*, Vol. XC, 2000, pp. 1–17; Zhmodikov, Alexander, 'Roman Republican Heavy Infantrymen in Battle,' *Historia*, Vol. 49, No. 1, 2000, pp. 67–78; and Lee, A.D., 'Morale and the Roman Experience of Battle,' Chapter 5 in Lloyd, Alan B. (ed.), *Battle in Antiquity*, The Classical Press of Wales, London, 1996, pp. 199–217. See also the relevant sections in Anglim, Simon et al., *Fighting Techniques of the Ancient World*, St. Martin's Press, New York, 2006; Carey, Brian T., *Warfare in the Ancient World*, Pen & Sword, Barnsley, 2005; and Warry, John, *Warfare in the Classical World*, University of Oklahoma Press, Norman, 1995.

Finally, there are the studies on the site of the battle of Philippi itself conducted by Heuzey, Léon, *Mission archéologique de Macédoine*, Paris, 1876, pp. 97–116, and Collart, Paul, 'Note sur les mouvements de troupes qui ont précéde la bataille de Philippes,' *Bulletin de Correspondance Hellenique*, Vol. 53, 1929, pp. 351–364. Their conclusions have been verified more recently by Kaïmaris, Georgoula, 'Photogrammetric and Photo Interpretation Research in the Plain of Philippi,' *Archaiologiko Ergo sti Makedonia kai Thraki*, Vol. 16, 2002, pp. 119–129. This article is written in the author's native language so, like Shakespeare's Casca, you may find yourself wryly conceding it's Greek to you too.

INDEX

References to illustrations are shown
in bold.

Adana 45
Africa 84, 86
Agrippa, Marcus Vipsanius 19, **80**, 81,
  83, 84, 85
Ahenobarbus, Gnaeus Domitius 48, 65,
  72, **73**, 78, 84, 86
Alba Fucens 11, 21, 82
Allienus 40, 91
Amanus Gates, battle of the (39 BC) 89, 91
Antigonus 90
Antiochus of Commagene 90, 91
Antonius, Gaius 39–40, **39**
Antonius, Lucius 79, **79**, 80, 82, 83,
  84, 86
Antony, Mark **16**, **75**, **84**
  alliance with Octavian 37
  and brother's death 40
  and Brutus's body 76
  and Caesar 6, 7–8, 18, **28**
  as commander 18–19, 22, **75**
  dramatic representations 93
  in the East 87–88, 90, 91
  at Forum Gallorum 29, 30, 31,
    32–34, 82
  journey to Philippi 48, 53, **55**
  and Murcus's blockade of Brundisium
    47
  at Mutina 34, 82
  negotiations with Sextus Pompey 82, 87
  peace treaty with Octavian 86
  and Perusine War 80, 82, 83, 84, 85
  at Philippi 54, 55–56, 61, **62–63** (64),
    68, 69, 73, 75, 76, 77
  Philippi aftermath 77, 79
  preparations for war 11–12
  provincial appointment 9–10
  relations with Octavian 8–9, 10–11
Apamea 6, 40, 88, 91
Aquila, Pontius 33, 34
Ariobarzanes, king of Cappadocia 45, 46
Athens 38, **38**
Augustus *see* Octavian

Bagradas River, battle of (49 BC) 24
ballistas **70–71** (72)
ballots 7
Bassus, Caecilius 5–6, 40
Bibulus, Lucius 49, 76–77
Bocchus II, king of Mauretania 84
Bogud, king of Mauretania 84
Bononia 12, 28, 34, 36, 82
Brundisium 47, 48, 78, 82, 85
Brundisium, Pact of (40 BC) 86
Brutus, Decimus
  as conspirator 7
  death 36
  fights with Antony for Gallia Cisalpina
    10, 11–12, 28, 34, 35
  flees Rome 8
Brutus, Lucius Junius 7

Brutus, Marcus Junius **17**, **48**, **49**, **76**
  in Athens 38
  as commander 16–17
  as conspirator 7
  dramatic representations **93**
  flees Rome 8
  journey to Philippi 48–49, **55**
  and Lycia 16, 44, 45–46, 91
  in Macedonia and Thrace 36–38
  at Philippi 51–52, 54–55, 56–60, 61–74
  provincial appointment 10

Caesar, Julius **5**, **6**
  assassination and funeral 7, 8, **9**,
    10, 33
  and civil wars 5–6
  as commander 24
  as dictator 5, 6–7
Caesar, Lucius 5
Caesarion 7, **37**
Calenus, Quintus Fufius 85
Calvinus, Domitius 65, 72
camps 21–22, **26**
Camulatus 73
Cannae, battle of (216 BC) 24
Carfulenus, Decimus 29, 32
Carrhae, battle of (53 BC) 6, 17
Carthage 5
Cassius Longinus, Gaius **18**, **76**
  burial 61
  camp at Philippi 50–51, 52, 53,
    62–63 (64)
  coins **49**
  as commander 17–18
  as conspirator 7
  in the East 40–46, 91
  flees Rome 8
  influence 69
  journey to Philippi 48–49, **55**
  at Philippi 54–55, 55–56, 57–61
  provincial appointment 10
Cassius Parmensis 41, 78
Cato, Marcus 74, 77
Censorinus, Marcius 85
Cicero, Marcus (orator's son) 38, 78
Cicero, Marcus Tullius 8, 11, 12, **33**,
  36, 37, 40
Cilicia 88, 89
Cimber, Tillius 8, 41–45, 48–49, 55
Cleopatra VII **37**
  and Antony 88, 90, 91
  and Caesar 7
  support for Triumvirs 41, 46, 47
Clodius, Gaius 39–40, 78
Cornificius, Quintus 48
Corsica 82, 84
Crassus, Publius Canidius 88
Crispus, Marcius 6, 40
Culāro 36, 82
Cyrrhestica, battle of (38 BC) 90, 91

Dante Alighieri 76
Deiotarus 39

Dolabella, Publius 7, 10, 38, 40–41,
  68, 91
Dyrrachium 39

Eastern theatre **91**
Egypt 41, 46, 47, 88, 91
Ephesus **85**, 87, 91

Fango, Fuficius 84
fortifications **62–63** (64)
Forum Gallorum, battle of (43 BC) 25, 29,
  30, **31**, 32–34, 82
Forum Julii 35
Forum Voconii 35, 82
Fulvia 37, 80, 83, 84, 85–86
Furnius, Gaius 80

Galba, Sulpicius 29–32
Gallia Cisalpina 9, 11, 12, 37, 82, 86
Gallia Comata 9, 12, 37
Gallia Narbonensis 35, 37, 86

Herod, King of the Jews 90, **90**, 91
Hirtius, Aulus 12, 28, 31, 32–33, 34
Horace 53, 75
Hortensius Hortalus 38, 39
Hybreas 88
Hyrcanus II, Ethnarch 90
Hyria 85

Italian theatre **82**

Jerusalem 90, **90**
Judea 40, 88, 89, 90, 91
Julia (Antony's mother) 84

Kavala *see* Neapolis

Labienus, Quintus 88, **88**, 89, 91
Laodicea 40–41, 91
Lentulus Spinther 41, 45, 46, 68
Lepidus, Marcus **36**
  African command 86
  aftermath of Caesar's death 8
  capabilities 36, 78
  joins Second Triumvirate 37
  and Mutina 33–34
  and Perusine War 80
  reconciliation with Antony 35–36, 82
lex Pedia 36
Livia Drusilla 77, 84
Lycians 16, 41, **42–43** (44), 46, 91

Macedonia 38–39
Masada **26**, **89**, 90
Menas 82, 84, 87
Messala Corvinus 57, 76–77
military tribunes 23, **23**
Misenum, Pact of (39 BC) 82, 87
Murcus, Lucius Statius **74**
  attempt on Cleopatra's fleet 46, 47
  off Brundisium 47, 48, 65, 72
  death 87

destroys Triumvirs' reinforcements 47, 65, 72
joins Cassius 40
joins Sextus Pompey 78
at Laodicea 41
in Syria 6
Mutina (Modena) 12, 18, 19, 28, 82
battle of (43 BC) 34, 82
Mylasa 88, 91
Myra 46

Naucrates 46
Neapolis (Kavala) 50, **50**, 92
Norbanus, Gaius 48–49, 53, 55
Nursia (Norcia) 80, 89

Octavia **84**, 86
Octavian, Gaius (later Emperor Augustus) **17, 34**
alliance with Mark Antony 37
attempted coup 11, 82
as commander 19
as consul 36
demands Caesar's inheritance 8–9
at Forum Gallorum 32
journey to Philippi 41, 54, **55**
march on Rome 36
negotiations with Sextus Pompey 82, 86–87
peace treaty with Antony 86
and Perusine War 80, 82, 84, 85
at Philippi 56–57, 61, 68, 75, 76, 77
preparations for war 12
relations with Mark Antony 8–9, 10–11
and Sicily 48
snubbed by Senate 34
veteran resettlement 79, 80
optimates 7, 17
Orodes II, king of Parthia 86, 88

Pacorus, Prince **87, 88, 89–90, 91**
Pansa, Gaius 12, 28–29, 31, 32, 34
Parthia and Parthians 6, 17, 88–90, 91
Patara 46
Perusia (Perugia) 80–83, **81**
Perusine War 79–87
Pharnaeus, Prince 89–90
Pharnastanes 89, 91
Philippi **51, 52**
approach to 48–49, 53, **55**
battle orders 53–54
bird's eye views **58–59, 66–67**
first battle 55–61, **60, 61, 62–63** (64)
government and history 49, 50
nowadays 92
opening moves 54–55
Republican camps and positions 50–52, **54, 57, 62–63** (64)
second battle 61–78, **74, 75**
Triumvirs' camps and positions 53, **56**
Triumvirs' loss of reinforcements 47, 65, **70–71** (72)
Phoenicia 88, 91
Plancus, Munatius
as governor of Asia 88

as governor of Gallia Comata 33, 34, 35, 36
and Perusine War 80, 81–83, 83–84
Pollentia (Pollenzo) 28, 33, 35, 82
Pollio, Asinius 6, 35, 36, 80, 81–83, 84, 86
Pompey the Great 5, 17, **19**
Pompey, Sextus **46**
fights Triumvirs 48, 78, 79
negotiations with Triumvirs 82, 86–87
rapprochement with Antony 84, 86
Senate gives supreme naval command to 34
in Spain 6
Porcia 77
praetorians 23

Republicans: symbols **48, 49**
Rhascupolis 49, 77
Rhascus 49, 75–76, 77
Rhodes 39, 40, 41, 45–46, 78, 91
Roman army
camps 21–22, **26**
cavalry 23
centurions 23
combat 23–25, 73
commanders and officers 23
drill 21
eagle standards **25**
legions *see below*
personal identification 23
political loyalties 27
recruitment 26–27
training 20–21
veteran arbitration attempt 83, 86
veteran resettlement 79–80
see also weapons
Roman army: legions 20, **20**, 22–23
II 11, 29, 34
III Gallica 53, 77
IV Macedonia 11, 12, 21, 33, 36, 53, 57, 77, 82
V Alaudae 11, 34, 77
VI Ferrata 11, 35, 53, 77
VII 11, 12, 33, 34, 53, 77, 79
VIII 11, 12, 34, 53, 77, 79
IX 11, 34
X Equestris 35, 53, 77
XII Fulmirata 24, 53, 77
XXVI 53, 79
XXVII 53
XXVIII 53
XXIX 53
XXX 53
XXXI 53
XXXIII 53
XXXV 11, 29, 30, 31, 34
XXXVI 53
XXXVII 53
Martian 11, 12, 21, 29, 32–33, 36, 72, 82
vernacular 27
Roman world **4**
Roman Republic: likelihood of longevity 78
Rome 36, 80, 81, 82, 86–87

Forum 7, **12, 33**
Pompey's Theatre 7, **8, 9**
Pons Fabricius **29**
Temple of Hercules Victor **32**
Temple of Portunus **32**
Rufus, Lucius 45
Rullus, Publius Servilius 85
Ruspina, battle of (46 BC) 24

Salvidienus Rufus, Quintus 48, 80, 82, 83, 86
Sambre, battle of (57 BC) 24
Samosata 90, 91
Sapaei Pass 49, **55**
Sardinia 82, 84
Saxa, Decidius 48–49, 53, 55, 88
Second Triumvirate 37, 82
senators **6**
senatus caligatus 27
Sentinum 80, 89
Serapio 41
Servilia 10, 76
Sextius, Titus 48, 84, 86
ships **68, 69, 70–71** (72)
Sicily 46, 47–48, 78, 82
Silanus, Marcus 33–34
Silo, Popaedius 89
Sipontum 82, 84, 85
Smyrna 40, 91
Spain **6**
standard-bearers **62–63** (64)
Stratonicea 88, 91
Syria 40–41, 88, 89–90

Tarsus 41–45, 88, 91
Taurus Mountains, battle of the (39 BC) 89, 91
testudines 24
Thrace 40
see also Philippi
Titinius 60
Trebonius, Caius 7, 8, 11, 38, 40
trumpeters **62–63** (64)
Turulius 78

Vada Sabatia 34–35, 82
Vatinius, Publius 39
Vegetius 21, 22, 23
Ventidius, Publius
and the Parthians 88–90, 91
and Perusine War 80, 81–83, 84
recruits troops for Antony 11, 12, 34, 35
Vetus, Antistius 6, 38
Via Egnatia 47, 48, 50, 51

Washington, Denzil **93**
weapons 65
daggers 9, 20, 48
shields 20, **22, 24**
slingbolts 83
spears 20, **21**
swords 20, **21**, 24

Xanthus, siege of (42 BC) 16, 41, **42–43** (44), 45, 46